Standards
PRIMER

PETER LANG
New York • Washington, D.C./Baltimore • Bern
Frankfurt am Main • Berlin • Brussels • Vienna • Oxford

Raymond A. Horn, Jr.

Standards
PRIMER

PETER LANG
New York • Washington, D.C./Baltimore • Bern
Frankfurt am Main • Berlin • Brussels • Vienna • Oxford

Library of Congress Cataloging-in-Publication Data

Horn, Raymond A.
Standards primer / Raymond A. Horn, Jr.
p. cm.
Includes bibliographical references.
1. Education—Standards—United States. I. Title.
LB3060.83.H67   379.1'58—dc22   2003027818
ISBN 0-8204-7078-3

Bibliographic information published by **Die Deutsche Bibliothek**.
Die Deutsche Bibliothek lists this publication in the "Deutsche
Nationalbibliografie"; detailed bibliographic data is available
on the Internet at http://dnb.ddb.de/.

Cover design by Lisa Barfield

The paper in this book meets the guidelines for permanence and durability
of the Committee on Production Guidelines for Book Longevity
of the Council of Library Resources.

© 2004 Peter Lang Publishing, Inc., New York
275 Seventh Avenue, 28th Floor, New York, NY 10001
www.peterlangusa.com

Printed in the United States of America

Table of Contents

CHAPTER ONE   Introduction   1

CHAPTER TWO   The Foundations of Standards   11

CHAPTER THREE   Technical Standards   63

CHAPTER FOUR   Standards of Complexity   93

CHAPTER FIVE   Conclusion   123

                   References and Resources   131

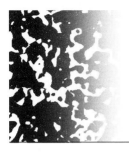

CHAPTER ONE

Introduction

Accountability

being responsible for one's actions within an educational system.

Standards

conceptual or factual criteria representing knowledge, skills, or attitudes that are established by an authority.

Educational stakeholders

all of the individuals who are affected by the activities of an educational system.

Each day the lives of public school administrators, teachers, students, and parents become more dominated by the current **standards** and **accountability** movement. Decisions that have severe consequences for all **educational stakeholders** and society are based upon mandated and voluntary standards and the assessments that hold all accountable for student achievement of the standards. In many schools, decisions involving whether students move from grade level to grade level, graduate from high school, or receive a professional certification are based on their mastery of standards as determined by a standardized test. Also in many schools, administrator and teacher job security and advancement contingent upon student achievement of the standards as determined by student test scores. Increasingly, public schools become vulnerable to privatization, loss of students and funding to school choice initiatives, or loss of autonomy due to unacceptable student mastery of the standards. Publishers of textbooks and instructional materials revamp their products to accommodate the standards and standardized tests. From kindergarten through

college, teachers and professors organize their lesson plans and syllabi around standards and focus their instruction on the content of the standardized test. Each year, millions of students take millions of tests based upon a wide range of standards. The efforts of the testing industry and the allocation of time and resources of the professional organizations and government agencies to develop, implement, and hold schools accountable for the standards now conservatively represent hundreds of millions of dollars per year. In short, standards and accountability now drive public education in America.

Most public school educators and the general public understand standards to be objective, value-neutral, and uncontroversial statements of agreed-upon knowledge and skills. Standards are promoted as essential knowledge and skills that have a direct effect on the national economy, national competitiveness in a global marketplace, and a student's future vocational and academic success. The efficient and effective assessment of standards is posed as objective standardized testing that can accurately determine school, educator, and student achievement of the standards. Through this allegedly accurate and efficient assessment, students and schools are compared and ranked in relation to student achievement of the standards. In addition, all stakeholders are held accountable for their effort in student mastery of the standards. The proposition is that the level of their accountability for the standardized test scores of the students can be efficiently determined, and punishments and rewards can be applied to spur greater accountability.

However, this view of standards as a generic concept and standardized tests as objective, value-neutral, and accurate determinants of student mastery of the standards is certainly not a complete or accurate picture. The nature of standards and the purpose and effectiveness of standardized testing as the sole determinant of student learning are far more complex phenomena than the simplistic representations that are made to the public. In fact there are many types of standards and assessments that represent diverse purposes and result in quite different consequences for all educational stakeholders and society. An understanding of the complexity of standards and accountability can inform the increasingly contentious debate over the current standards and

accountability reform. As more individuals are affected by the implementation of this reform, understanding the diverse views on standards and accountability through assessment becomes a critical activity.

The purpose of this primer is to provide a deeper and broader understanding of this major reform of American education in order for individuals to critique their assumptions about the nature and consequences of all standards and accountability positions. To facilitate this purpose, the *Standards Primer* will discuss two distinctly different categories of standards and accountability—technical standards and standards of complexity. Chapter Two will deal with foundational information concerning these two views. Following a discussion of the history of standards in America, the important issues of who makes the standards, who should make the standards, and the relevance of standards will be discussed. The many types of standards and the two essential categories of standards—technical standards and standards of complexity will be identified. Chapters Three and Four discuss both of these essential categories in relation to their effects on curriculum, instruction, and assessment. Chapter Five discusses the consequences and implications of technical standards and standards of complexity. Chapter Six provides additional references for the reader. These chapters will provide a comprehensive understanding of educational standards by examining the origins of standards, by expanding the contextual knowledge of standards, and by identifying and critiquing the hidden patterns in which both of the essential views of standards are embedded and that arise out of each view.

However, the following discussion first will provide general information on standards and curriculum, standards and instruction, and standards and assessment.

Standards and Curriculum

To most individuals, curriculum is simply defined as the organization of the content and skills that are to be learned. Curriculum development then becomes a matter of deciding which facts, opinions, and values are important enough to be learned and which skills are needed in the acquisition of this content. However, a more complex consideration of curriculum must

include an understanding of epistemology. **Epistemology** is the study of knowledge and includes various types of knowledge (such as formally validated knowledge and indigenous knowledge), the acquisition of knowledge (such as the transmission of knowledge by experts or the discovery and construction of knowledge by students), the social reproduction of selected knowledge, and the consequences of the use and acquisition of knowledge. Epistemological questions would include: What constitutes valid knowledge? Who produces knowledge? How is knowledge acquired? What are the consequences of knowledge?

These are important questions because, as Joe L. Kincheloe (2001b) points out, epistemology "invisibly shapes not only the form school takes but also the way we think, our consciousness, the way we see the world, our images of ourselves, even our own identities. Indeed, epistemology matters as it shapes us and the world around us" (p. 325). Central to a discussion of technical standards and standards of complexity is how each view of standards answers the previous questions. How they are answered shapes us in all the ways that Kincheloe identified.

Standards and Instruction

To ensure student learning, all types of standards are aligned with instructional techniques that promote the philosophy in which the standards are grounded. An examination of how the standards are delivered to the students also uncovers the essential differences between the different views on standards. A comprehensive examination of the instructional component of learning must include all of the elements of the instructional system. These elements include instructional methods, instructional technology, the instructional schedule, the role of the teacher, the teacher's professional development relating to instruction, how the instructional philosophy mediates the definition of teacher professionalism, and the role of the administration as it relates to instruction. In schools that have integrated their educational philosophy throughout the learning process, that philosophy not only will be evident within the curriculum, instruction, and assessment components of the school but also within each of the elements of the instructional system.

Standards and Assessment

In any educational system, the function of assessment is to determine how well the system's philosophical purposes have been implemented. Ideally, the philosophical purposes are achieved through an alignment of curriculum, instruction, and assessment, in that each of these components of the learning process is guided by the philosophy that drives the process. The mantra of the current educational reform movement—standards, accountability, and testing—is indicative of this alignment. Educators and students are held accountable for the learning of technical standards by the results of a standardized test. An emphasis on standardized testing as an accountability measure has a long history and a pervasive presence in American education. Besides the well-known achievement tests such as the SAT, ACT, and GRE, many industries utilize standardized tests to rank and sort potential employees and to gauge an individual's ability or suitability. However, there are other types of assessments that perform similar and different functions. The fundamental difference of different types of assessments is reflected in the multiple purposes of assessment.

The *purposes of assessment* can include providing feedback on instructional effectiveness, measuring student ability, improving student learning, comparing students and schools, and providing an accountability mechanism to determine educator effectiveness. Due to the differences among these purposes, it is difficult for one assessment instrument to capture this diversity of purpose. In fact, if the purpose is to measure achievement of the standards, a single test only provides a snapshot of selected portions of the complete standards. Also, some groups such as the National Forum on Assessment argue that all assessment, regardless of purpose must be fair to all students, strengthened by professional collaboration and development, developed and monitored with broad community involvement, supported by systematic and clear communication, and regularly reviewed and improved (Neill, 2000, p. 102).

However, the strongest component of the current standards reform movement is *accountability* as determined by the results of standardized testing. The idea has been extensively promoted that test scores can measure the quality of education. An implied

assumption that provides a foundation for this idea is that educational quality is determined by the degree in which individuals fulfill their personal responsibility as teachers and learners in the mastery of the standards as determined by their performance on a standardized test. This assumption minimizes or denies that collective decisions and social conditions play a part in the determination of educational quality. In educational systems that are test focused, accountability for teaching and learning is individual not social. Many opponents of the use of single assessments argue that this individualistic focus is a smoke screen that hides the real causes of low educational quality, which are significantly more difficult to resolve. Causes such as low and inequitable funding of schools, racist policies, and the control of public education by special interests require complex, expensive, and politically unpopular solutions. Therefore, low educational quality is proposed as a systemwide condition caused by a lack of individual accountability that can be quickly, easily, and cheaply corrected through the construction of technical standards assessed by a high-stakes standardized test.

Outside of the standardized testing culture, many *different types of assessment* are recognized. Assessment generally can be objective, written, or authentic. *Analytic models* of assessment assume that small chunks of student performance of a standard can accurately represent the students' understanding of the whole standard. Analytic models, such as objective tests, do not require interpretation because they consist of multiple-choice, matching, true/false, short-answer, and fill-in questions. However, they are not objective in the sense of being value neutral because the values of the test constructor affect what content is validated as the only right answer. Also, objective tests are the most efficient types of assessment in providing quick statistical data that can be used for comparison purposes. Written tests, such as essay tests, are less efficient for comparative purposes and invite test taker interpretation. Written tests can range from open-ended writing opportunities for the test taker, to highly structured writing activities that culminate in a predetermined correct answer. Determination of a correct answer or correct writing format is more complicated because of issues involving the amount that is written, the quality of the writing, and whether different raters can arrive at the same conclusion about a student's essay. Also,

assessment that uses analytical models tends to rely on one test to determine student achievement. The assessment strategy that is characteristic of current technical standards systems is analytical.

An additional type of assessment that provides an alternative to analytical models of testing is **authentic assessment**. Authentic assessments test students' knowledge and skills as they would be applied in real-life situations. *Holistic models* of assessment, such as authentic assessment, represent the belief that assessment of the student's performance of a standard must include the complete standard rather than only one or more parts of the standard. Authentic assessments are in the form of performance assessments that assess individual student performances of content and skills in the areas of writing, science, math, visual arts, oral communications, language arts, and social studies. They could be in the form of oral presentations, written communications, experiments, projects, or any other activity that requires the use of the knowledge and skills identified in the standards. Rubrics that specifically detail the required knowledge and skills can be used as diagnostic or evaluative assessments of the students' mastery of the standards. In holistic models of assessment, student achievement of standards associated with individual subjects or with multiple subjects in an interdisciplinary activity can be assessed through the use of portfolios. The use of holistic models of assessment is a commitment to the use of multiple forms of assessment to capture the complete picture of a student's mastery of the standards. Standards, as constructed in standards of complexity systems, may be more conceptual than specific in identifying what a student is to learn. In this case, holistic models are utilized to create real-life situations in which students demonstrate their skill in the construction of knowledge.

Also, assessment can be viewed as norm referenced or criterion referenced. Basically, in *norm-referenced assessment*, student performance of a standard is compared to the performances of other students. Individual students can be compared to the average score of other students in the class, school, school district, state, or nation. However, norm-referenced assessment only identifies how well a student did in relation to other student performances. It does not necessarily determine whether a student mastered the standard or is ready to advance to another standard, class, or grade level. Norm-referenced tests such as the Iowa Test

Authentic assessment
assessment of student learning within the context of real-life problems and situations.

of Basic Skills do not measure student achievement. They only measure a sampling of knowledge and skills relevant to a specific grade level. Conversely, *criterion-referenced assessment* compares the student performance to a performance standard. In this case, how well other students performed is not relevant. Criterion-referenced assessment is most often used when basic skills are being taught. Criterion-referenced assessment can take the form of a standardized test or a scoring rubric. Student achievement of the standards or the criteria can be determined by a raw score, a percentage, or a scaled score that makes comparisons across tests possible (Wilde, 2002, p. 10). However, criterion-referenced tests can become norm-referenced tests. Susan Wilde (2002) points out that "if passing scores end up being determined not by an objective judgment of how one knows whether a criterion has been reached but instead by what proportion of students should, for political reasons, be allowed to have passed, a criterion-referenced measure has metamorphosed into a norm-referenced one" (p. 10). Wilde and others further suggest that these tests should be called politically referenced tests. Both technical standards and standards of complexity can utilize both norm-referenced and criterion-referenced assessments in the identification of student achievement.

Finally, the current technical standards assessment climate is narrowly focused on standardized tests in which **high-stakes exit level tests** are quickly becoming the norm. High-stakes exit level testing implies that there is a significant consequence for the students who do not perform at acceptable levels on the standardized test. These consequences may include not passing to the next grade, not graduating, or not receiving a professional certification. In addition, schools may lose funding, be privatized, lose students through school choice options, or be taken over by a state government. Educators may have their job security, professional advancement, or salaries affected by student test scores. Currently, this push for high-stakes testing often does *not* include a substantial public debate on the consequences of this type of testing on educational stakeholders or the educational community. Because of these consequences, numerous opponents of high-stakes standardized tests (Bracey, 1998, 2000, 2002; Berliner & Biddle, 1996; Horn, 2001a, 2001b, 2002; McNeil, 2000; Ohanian, 1999; Orfield & Kornhaber, 2001; Popham, 2001; Sacks, 1999; Swope

High-stakes exit level test

when individuals pass a standardized test in order to move to the next educational level, complete a program, or receive a professional certification.

& Miner, 2000a; Wilde, 2002) pose a diversity of arguments against the use of this type of assessment. Daniel M. Koretz (1995) captures some of the essentials arguments in opposition to the use of high-stakes tests to ensure accountability to educational standards:

- High-stakes testing often produces an illusion of accountability and an illusion of progress.
- The flip side of the focus on the content of a high-stakes test is a narrowing of instruction.
- Teaching to the test often degrades instruction.
- The tests that most reformers want to use—various types of performance assessments—face some formidable technical obstacles.
- As commonly administered, most tests reveal virtually nothing about the quality of schools.
- Many reform proposals establish too many and often conflicting—goals for assessments.
- Excessive emphasis on testing and test-based accountability diverts attention from other problems, some of which are severe and pressing. (pp. 156–160)

Glossary

Accountability—being responsible for one's actions within an educational system.

Authentic assessment—assessment of student learning within the context of real-life problems and situations.

Educational stakeholders—all of the individuals who are affected by the activities of an educational system.

Epistemology—the study of the acquisition of knowledge, the social reproduction of selected knowledge, and the consequences of the acquisition and use of knowledge.

High-stakes exit level test— a standardized test that must be passed in order to move to the next educational level, complete a program, or receive a professional certification.

Standards—conceptual or factual criteria representing knowledge, skills, or attitudes that are established by an authority.

The Foundations of Standards

Introduction

Media discussions about standards suggest that standards are generic in that a standard is a standard; however, even in a cursory study of educational standards, it soon becomes apparent that there are many types of standards. Standards are the basis for the validation of an individual's degree of competence in the performance of a specific activity or in a specific field or occupation. Successful performance of the standards assures us of or validates the individual's ability to provide expert performance of the standards on some level.

Assurance of the mastery of the standards is provided through the processes of credentialing, licensure, and certification. *Credentialing standards* tell us about an individual's qualifications in relation to the individual's knowledge and ability within a disciplinary or occupational context. Educational diplomas, grade-point average, and class rank are examples of devices that indicate the degree of individual attainment of standards. *Licensure standards* involve credentialing by a government entity that allows the indi-

vidual to engage in some sort of professional activity with a degree of authority. To legally engage in many professional activities, individuals need to be licensed by a governmental body after demonstrating mastery of the professional standards. *Standards of Certification,* granted by either a professional organization or a government entity, authorize an individual to use a title or other designation as an indicator of the individual's authority and professionalism within a designated area. In our lives, we often seek out the credentialed, licensed, and certified individuals to provide us with goods and services. Our society values credentialing, licensure, and certification because some professional or governmental organization guarantees that these individuals have successfully met certain standards within their field. This assures us that our chances of receiving expert or professionally informed service are greater with the credentialed, licensed, or certified individual than with others who have not been so validated.

However, on another level, the expertise, professionalism, and specialized knowledge of the validated individual may vary in relation to the *type* of standard that is the focus of the validation process. The different types of standards tell us different things about what an individual has learned and what that individual can do. This chapter will explore the different types of standards that that are involved in the validation process used in educational contexts. However, to understand the significance of the different types and categories of standards requires foundational knowledge about the following:

- The history of standards.
- Who makes standards?
- Who should make the standards?
- The many types of standards.
- The two essential categories of standards.

The History of Standards

In a global context, the establishment of educational standards and the use of standardized testing to determine student achievement can be traced back to the ancient Chinese. However, in American education, Horace Mann, as secretary of the Massachusetts Board of Education, instituted the first use of standardized exams in public schools. In response to the diversity of the population caused by extensive immigration, Mann worked to establish a mandatory school system that would ensure social stability by promoting common values and beliefs. Mann believed that public support and public control of the common school could achieve this goal. Beginning in the 1830s, the middle and upper classes envisioned education as the means to forestall social unrest and to create a literate society that would ensure a productive labor force. The assumption was that by providing free education for the children of the poor and disadvantaged, common values, beliefs, and knowledge could be promoted in society. Generally, as a social control mechanism, the free common school proved to be very effective and enduring.

The Early 1900s

The Committee of Ten

The philosophical difference between the two current views of standards was formally expressed in the findings of two turn-of-the-century committees that explored the purpose of education. In 1893, to provide a guiding vision for American education, the National Education Association convened the Committee of Ten, chaired by Charles W. Eliot, president of Harvard University. The Committee of Ten recommended that a national curriculum consisting of a mixture of classical and modern courses should be provided for all high school students (Kliebard, 1995). The essence of the report was that there would be no difference in the curriculum taken by those who would go to college and those students who would enter the workforce. This curriculum was devoid of any vocational preparation because the Committee thought that all occupational decisions should be postponed until after graduation. Eliot reasoned that the development of all students would be enhanced with the study of classic and modern language, mathematics, literature, science, and history. The current technical view of standards reflects the Committee's recommendations in that standards should be developed that specifically reflect each subject area rather than reflect an integration of the subjects or an interdisciplinary construction of the standards. In reflecting upon the recommendations of the Committee of Ten, Tucker and Codding (1998) cite that currently "a rising chorus

is calling for a return to the demands of the core disciplines and the idea that all students should meet a common high academic standard before going their separate ways" (p. 74). In addition, since the inception of the College Entrance Examination Board in 1900, college entrance requirements have emphasized a traditional course of study involving math, languages, literature, history, and, later, the natural sciences (Bracey, 2002, p. 38), thus, reinforcing the original intent of the Committee of Ten.

The Cardinal Principles of Education

However, in 1918, another committee commissioned by the National Education Association presented their findings as The Cardinal Principles of Education. These principles, which would guide secondary education curriculum for most of the 20th century, were focused on the development and socialization of the individual into American society. The problem with how high schools were conducted involved the fact that all students were being prepared to go to college, an outcome that few would actually realize. In addition, economic necessity drove many students out of the high school before graduation. Questions were raised concerning how to create a more relevant curriculum for the non-college students. In opposition to the emphasis on academic subjects, the Cardinal Principles included seven aims that would guide the curriculum: health, command of fundamental processes, worthy home membership, vocation, citizenship, worthy use of leisure, and the development of ethical character. In addition, in 1917 the Smith-Hughes Act provided federal support for vocational education, home economics, and agricultural education in the public schools. This legislation moved the American curriculum in a direction away from the academic emphasis suggested by the Committee of Ten. This broader definition of curriculum and the emphasis on the student and the effect of the larger environment on the student are antecedents of standards of complexity.

The Social Efficiency Movement and the Scientific Management of Education

Concurrently, the influence of the business community and business practice in education formally began with the publica-

tion of Frederick Winslow Taylor's (1911) book, *The Principles of Scientific Management.* Taylor's ideas along with those of Edward A. Ross and John Franklin Bobbitt (1918) become known as the Social Efficiency Movement in education (Kliebard, 1995). The Social Efficiency Movement resulted in a hierarchical and hegemonic educational structure that at best mimicked and in some cases replicated the routinization, specialization, and bureaucratization of the business community (Bennett & LeCompte, 1990). Proponents of this movement saw the organization and procedures that led to the material success of the American business community as directly applicable to education. Gerald Bracey (2002) connects this early attempt of business to influence education with the current standards and accountability reforms in his comment that "the press for efficiency in the early years of the twentieth century had its reprise in calls for higher standards and higher skills in the century's last two decades" (p. 38).

The empirical tradition of experimental science, as espoused by the behavioral psychologists of this time period, enhanced the **scientific management of schools.** Thorndike, the leading behaviorist, believed that all human experience could be quantified through statistical analysis. Also, in the early 1900s, the rise of intelligence testing greatly affected education. The work of individuals such as Francis Galton, Charles Spearman, Alfred Binet, and Louis Terman promoted the mental measurement of children. Spurred by the Army Tests during World War I under the direction of Robert Yerkes, the widespread use of intelligence testing became a device for the sorting of individuals in relation to placing students into their "proper" slots in the school system (Sacks, 1999, p. 73). For a detailed discussion of intelligence testing at this time see Peter Sacks's (1999), *Standardized Minds,* and Stephen Gould's (1981), *The Mismeasure of Man.* In 1994, building upon the work of Arthur Jensen (1974, 1980), Herrnstein and Murray, in *The Bell Curve,* once again made the case for the ranking and sorting of individuals through the use of intelligence testing. For a critique of *The Bell Curve,* see Kincheloe, Steinberg, and Gresson (1996) *Measured Lies: The Bell Curve Examined.* The current use of standardized testing to measure the mastery of standards is directly related to the Social Efficiency Movement, the influence of behavioral psychology, and the influence of intelligence testing. The disciplinary nature of the standards that would

Scientific management of schools

the use and dominance of scientific and business principles in educational organization, management, teaching, and learning.

be efficiently taught and tested is directly tied to the conclusions of the Committee of Ten.

The Progressive Movement in Education

However, the Progressive Education Association contested this view of education. This association represented different beliefs about education, but commonality lay in the focus on the child instead of on academic disciplines. The association promoted the Seven Principles of progressive education: freedom to develop naturally; interest, the motive of all work; the teacher a guide, not a taskmaster; scientific study of pupil development; greater attention to all that affects the child's physical development; co-operation between school and home to meet the needs of the child's life; and, the progressive school, a leader in educational movements (Kliebard, 1995). The influence of the association was seen small group activities, more interesting curriculum materials, and in the use of playgrounds and gymnasiums. John Dewey represented a different progressive philosophy that was pragmatically child centered. He agreed that the interests of children, and children as active learners, were essential elements in the learning process; however, he also believed that reflective thinking and problem solving must mediate a child's interaction with the environment. Dewey maintained that educational growth involved a constant reflective interaction with the experience that a student encounters. Dewey disagreed with the efficiency considerations of standardization, precise measurement of standards, and any pedagogy that ignored the social consequences of a child's education (Horn, 2002). Besides Dewey's concerns about the social efficiency of education, Raymond E. Callahan (1962) later provided a classic criticism of the scientific management of schools in his book *Education and the Cult of Efficiency*. Proponents of standards of complexity systems trace their origins to the progressive and pragmatic view of John Dewey.

The 1960s: The ESEA and the NAEP

Two pieces of legislation in the 1960s have had a continuing effect on standards and accountability reforms. In 1965, as part of Lyndon Johnson's Great Society anti-poverty program,

Title I of the Elementary and Secondary Education Act (ESEA) was passed. The ESEA was legislation that provided federal funding for schools for the purposes of improving education for all children, helping children break the cycle of poverty, and fighting inequality in the schools. To ensure that schools would be accountable to the goals of the ESEA, Congress has required schools to evaluate and report on their effectiveness in meeting the ESEA requirements. A common practice adopted by schools to measure their outcomes was the use of standardized tests. Because of their reliance on federal funding, schools greatly increased their use of standardized testing. The current reliance on standardized tests to measure accountability came from the idea that "if standardized achievement tests could ascertain the effectiveness of ESEA-funded, basic skills-focused instructional programs, they could be employed to evaluate the success of other types of instructional programs as well" (Popham, 2001, p. 9).

An additional federal influence on the use of standardized testing to determine accountability is the National Assessment of Educational Progress test (NAEP), America's report card. In 1967, Congress mandated this test to provide information on student achievement in various subjects, including reading, writing, mathematics, and science. Even though it is the closest thing that we have to a national test, the NAEP is not tied to a particular curriculum model. Through the years this test has provided large amounts of data on student achievement that can be accessed through the National Center for Statistical Data (see Chapter Six). Initially, the NAEP was restricted to only providing scores by region. However, in 1988, Congress amended the law to allow for state-by-state reporting. Because it does not measure a specific curriculum, the NAEP is loosely connected to what happens in classrooms (Bracey, 2002). Also, NAEP data have been used to support the positions of both proponents and opponents of technical standards systems that employ standardized testing. Currently, the NAEP serves as a check on the scores of individual state tests. In addition, the NAEP provides a significant precedent for the proponents of the use of standardized testing to determine student achievement and school effectiveness.

The 1970s and 1980s

In the 1970s as the United States economy deteriorated and experienced stagflation (when recession and inflation are evident at the same time), the business community and politicians focused the blame on the public schools (Cremin, 1989). For this and other reasons, some states initiated educational reforms that focused on the development of statewide standards and accountability testing. Notably, Michigan instituted the Michigan Accountability System that used mandatory statewide testing as its basic tool to determine accountability for student learning. In the late 1970s, Texas began a standards and accountability reform focused on state standards and accountability testing that continues to evolve to the present. In fact, with the election of George W. Bush and the selection of Ron Paige, former superintendent of the Houston Independent School District, the Texas reform model became the basis for the No Child Left Behind Act of 2001. Cases like the educational reforms of Kentucky, Michigan, Texas, and other states promoted the idea that "taxpayer funding of schools should be preceded by proof of educational efficiency" (Sacks, 1999, p. 78).

With the conservative restoration that occurred with the election of Ronald Reagan in 1980, educational effectiveness became the focus of educational reform. Excellence not equity would be the catchword. A basic tenet of this conservative view on education, that would guide the reform of education, included a belief in individual responsibility and accountability rather than a collective responsibility for individual and societal problems. In addition, there was a return to the belief that the purpose of education is directly linked to the economic and business needs of the nation. Accordingly, American education was represented as inefficient and ineffective. Social promotion and grade inflation became issues that allegedly attested to the failure of American schools. In 1983, the National Commission on Excellence in Education, directed by Education Secretary Terrance Bell, proclaimed that not only had American education failed the country but that the threat was so great from this educational mediocrity that "if an unfriendly foreign power had attempted to impose on America the mediocre educational performance that exists today, we might well have viewed it as an act of war"

(National Commission on Excellence in Education 1983, p. 5). Through the 1980s, dozens of commissions issued reports citing the failures of education and proclaiming their own solutions (Ornstein & Hunkins, 1998, pp. 163–168).

1989 to the Present

The current standards and accountability movement began in earnest in 1989 when President George Bush convened an Educational Summit in Charlottesville, Virginia, with the nation's governors, including Governor Bill Clinton. By 1991, the results of this summit were formally proposed to Congress as *America 2000*. Six national goals were proposed that would be achieved through a fifteen-item Accountability Package, which called for a new national exam known as the American Achievement Test (Bush, 1991). The standardized test was to be a voluntary nationwide examination on five core subjects and tied to the World Class Standards that would be developed by the National Education Goals Panel (Bush, 1991). In addition, "colleges will be urged to use the American Achievement Tests in admissions and employers will be urged to pay attention to them in hiring" (Bush, 1991, p. 13). Congress did not approve *America 2000*; however, in 1991 and 1992 the Department of Education in collaboration with the National Endowment for the Humanities and the National Science Foundation awarded grants to professional organizations to develop voluntary national standards in seven school subjects (science, history, geography, the arts, civics, foreign languages, and English (Ravitch, 2000, p. 432). Prior to this the National Council of Teachers of Mathematics had already constructed its own standards.

When released, the voluntary standards met serious opposition from conservative groups. For instance, Lynne V. Cheney blasted the history standards (National Center for History in the Schools, 1994) as politically biased and negative toward the United States and the West in general (Cheney, 1994; Nash, Crabtree, & Dunn, 2000; Symcox, 2002). The English standards that were constructed by the International Reading Association (IRA) and the National Council of Teachers of English (NCTE) fared no better (Allington, 2002; NCTE & IRA, 1996). They were sharply criticized for their alleged lack of attention to correct usage, traditional literature, and their emphasis on process

over content. By 1995, the National Council of Teachers of Mathematics (1989) standards were vilified as the "new new math" and the fuzzy math because of their emphasis on higher-order thinking and problem solving rather than on basic skills. Conservative attacks continued on any standards that were constructivist oriented. The attack on the whole language movement personified the clash between constructivists who promoted process and student-centered learning and traditionalists who promoted content and teacher-directed learning (Chall, 1967, 2000; Goodman, 1986).

In 1994, President Clinton provided a boost to the standards and accountability movement with his Educate America Act (United States Congress, 1994). The provisions of this legislation, known as Goals 2000, were similar to Bush's America 2000 in that they called for Americans to be first in science and mathematics achievement and the establishment of a National Education Standards and Improvement Council (NESIC), whose task was to certify and review voluntary national standards and state content standards in the basic academic subjects. Opponents of the development of national standards later attacked NESIC as a "national school board" that violated traditions of local control (Berkson, 1997). In 1997, President Clinton continued to promote the idea of national standards and testing when he proposed a Call to Action for American Education. When this initiative failed to gain congressional approval, in 1999 Clinton proposed a similar plan to promote standards and accountability through testing in his Education Accountability Act. In the 2000 presidential election, education policy was not significantly debated because of the similarity of the Bush, Clinton, and Gore positions.

The standards and accountability reforms that had been developing for two decades finally became law with the passage of the No Child Left Behind Act of 2001 (NCLB). This law requires all states to develop high achievement standards and an accountability system to measure student achievement of the standards. Specifically, by the 2005–2006 school year, all children must be tested in grades 3–8 and not less than once during the tenth and twelfth grade to ensure student progress in meeting the standards. By 2014 all students must perform at the proficient level in reading and math. The states have the responsibility to

meet these and the other NCLB requirements; however, each state must submit its compliance plan to the U.S. Department of Education for approval. In order to avoid federal sanctions, states are developing severe consequences for schools that do not comply with the state plan to meet the NCLB requirements. For instance, Pennsylvania identifies schools that do not meet their yearly testing targets as Identified for Improvement (IFI). The following actions may be taken if there is a lack of adequate yearly progress in student test scores:

- Giving parents the option of transferring their children to another school within the school district.
- Requiring supplemental services to be provided by the school district in tutoring and remedial instruction for low-income families.
- Replacing staff who are deemed relevant to the failure.
- Instituting and implementing new curriculum.
- Appointing an outside advisor.
- Restructuring the organization of the school.
- Converting to a charter school.
- Turning the operation of the school over to the state can then privatize the school or place its control under an appointed entity.

Because of these penalties many school districts are instituting instruction that is focused on the test content and are voluntarily creating high-stakes consequences for students who fail the tests. This focus on teaching to the test is in opposition to research that supports pedagogical **best practice** and **multiple assessment**. Richard F. Elmore (2003) attempts to explain how the NCLB precipitates regressive pedagogical practice that is focused on a single standardized assessment measure by identifying design flaws in NCLB such as overinvestment in testing accompanied by an underinvestment in capacity building, ungrounded theories of school improvement, weak knowledge about how to turn around weak schools, perverse incentives for quality and performance, and policymaking by remote control.

Best practice
curriculum, instruction, and assessment that can be supported by quantitative and qualitative research.

Multiple assessment
the use of multiple techniques in the measurement of student achievement.

The Influence of Business on Educational Policy

One pattern that emerged from the commissions of the 1980s was the refocusing of the purpose of education on the

needs of the business sector. Because of the conservative focus on business, many of the commissions predominately consisted of business leaders, politicians, and educators who agreed with this focus on the needs of business. The increasing influence of business in education was best epitomized by the Texas reforms. In 1983, the governor of Texas appointed Ross Perot to chair a task force called the Select Committee on Public Education. Perot's reform attitude was summarized in his statement "we've got to drop a bomb on them, we've got to nuke them—that's the way you change these organizations" (McNeil, 2000, p. 153). In 1984, Perot's committee's recommendations were passed by the Texas legislature and included increased graduation requirements, a no-pass, no-play measure for student athletes, the requirement for each student to pass an exit-level competency test in order to receive a school diploma, and a maximum five-day absence rule per semester. In addition, the legislature mandated a statewide curriculum framework for each grade level and subject area. Linda McNeil (2000) characterizes the Texas reforms as "driven from the top, defined as management problems waiting for an expert manager to solve. They were formulated on the assumption that schools are at the bottom of the bureaucracy" (p. 153).

Throughout the 1990s, business continued to influence educational policy. In 1989, the National Center on Education and the Economy (NCEE) (1998) provided a team to participate in a fact-finding mission to Europe and Asia with the Commission on the Skills of the American Workplace. In 1990, greatly influenced by the German and Japanese educational systems, the Commission proposed a Certificate of Initial Mastery (CIM) in its report, *America's Choice: High Skills or Low Wages.* Designed to address the dual problems of low expectations and lack of motivation, the commission proposed that we should adopt the best instruction and curriculum practices of other countries, "the generic skills required to be successful in the modern workplace" (Tucker & Codding, 1998, p. 39), and create a certificate that reflects those standards. This proposed certificate would be different from a high school diploma in that "where we now award a diploma for time spent in school, we would instead award a certificate for reaching a predetermined—high—level of measured achievement" (Tucker & Codding, 1998, p. 39). In addition, the NCEE Workforce Development program "provides assistance in the development of strong state and local standards-based school-to-work transition systems with real employer involvement; it also helps to link these programs to statewide workforce development systems" (Tucker & Codding, 1998, p. 252). A related proposal involved the creation of a national basic skills certificate (NBSC) in which in grade ten students would demonstrate that they had "the mathematical and language skills necessary to achieve good jobs in the American economy" by passing a series of exams related to basic academic skills in these areas (Berkson, 1997, p. 208). Critics of the idea of mastery certificates such as CIM and NBSC argue that they are an attempt to replace the academic diploma, artificially lower the higher dropout rates caused by high-stakes testing, and push some students out of school at grade ten-making them available as cheap labor (Ohanian, 2000).

In 1996, a Second National Education Summit, at the IBM Palisades Conference Center took place. Hosted by the CEOs of IBM, AT&T, Proctor & Gamble, Boeing, Bell South, Eastman Kodak, other business leaders, and the National Governors' Association, the conference outcome was a commitment from the attending governors to produce state standards. This position, which reflected the conservative opinion that standards should be developed on a state and local level, not by the national government, is not surprising since numerous conservatives and conservative think tanks were invited as resources including Lynn Cheney, American Enterprise Institute; Denis Doyle, Heritage Foundation; Chester Finn, Hudson Institute; Diane Ravitch, consultant; Albert Shanker, American Federation of Teachers; Lewis Solmon, Milken Foundation; and Bob Schwartz, Pew Charitable Trusts (Ohanian, 2000, p. 352).

In addition, business organizations such as the Business Roundtable (1996), an association of chief executive officers, suggest, "that standards should reflect the academic skills and knowledge that students will need once they are in the workforce. Also, business leaders as well as the general public should be involved in the writing and reviewing of state standards" (Thurlow & Ysseldyke, 2001, p. 388). In addition, the "Business Roundtable noted that standards should be tied to effective assessments, and that these standards should be comparable to or higher than

standards from other nations" (Thurlow & Ysseldyke, 2001, pp. 388–389).

Alfie Kohn and Patrick Shannon (2002) provide a detailed discussion of the direct influence of business in schools in *Education, Inc.: Turning Learning into a Business.* Detailed information is provided about how this influence is manifested in program and activity sponsorships, exclusive agreements, incentive programs, the appropriation of space, sponsorship of educational materials, electronic marketing, privatization, fund raising, Channel One, test-prep marketing, business grants, and food services. Another source, Kenneth J. Saltman's (2000) book *Collateral Damage: Corporatizing Public Schools—A Threat to Democracy,* generally examines corporate influence on public education but also details the case of Coca-Cola's involvement in schools.

Points of Contention

The decades-long attempt to institute a technical standards and standardized testing system is based upon certain assumptions. Opponents of this type of standards and accountability system continuously contest these assumptions and propose that they are actually myths. The following is a compilation of these assumptions/myths.

- Testing will enhance productivity (Kornhaber & Orfield, 2001, p. 5).
- Testing will motivate students (Kornhaber & Orfield, 2001, p. 7).
- Testing will improve teaching and learning (Kornhaber & Orfield, 2001, p. 9).
- American schools are in peril (Sacks, 1999, p. 82).
- The U.S. economy is in peril because of an inferior education system (Sacks, 1999, p. 84).
- Greater school accountability will mean higher achievement (Sacks, 1999, p. 87).
- Student achievement has recently fallen across the nation (Berliner & Biddle, 1995, p. 13).
- College-student performance has recently declined in America (Berliner & Biddle, 1995, p. 35).
- Myths about intelligence: Such as students are dumber today than they used to be; student intelligence is determined only

by inheritance; and, student intelligence is largely fixed before students enter school (Berliner & Biddle, 1995, p. 41).

- American schools fail in comparative studies of student achievement (Berliner & Biddle, 1995, p. 51).
- America spends a lot more money on education than other countries (Berliner & Biddle, 1995, p. 66).
- Money is not related to school achievement (Berliner & Biddle, 1995, p. 70); or, the master myth that money does-n't matter (Bracey, 2002, p. 18).
- Costs in education have recently skyrocketed wastefully (Berliner & Biddle, 1995, p. 78).
- American schools are generally incompetent (Berliner & Biddle, 1995, p. 87).
- American schools do not produce workers with good technical skills (Berliner & Biddle, 1995, p. 88).
- American workers are not productive, and the schools are at fault (Berliner & Biddle, 1995, p. 92).
- American education doesn't produce enough scientists, mathematicians, and engineers (Berliner & Biddle, 1995, p. 95).
- Those who enter teaching have little ability and receive a poor academic education (Berliner & Biddle, 1995, p. 102).
- American citizens are unhappy with their schools (Berliner & Biddle, 1995, p. 111).

For another detailed discussion of these myths, see Gerald W. Bracey's (1997) *Setting the Record Straight: Responses to Misconceptions about Public Education in the United States.*

Who Makes Standards?

Understanding the distinction between the different types of standards requires knowing who makes the standards. The connection between the type of standard and the creator of the standards is important because the type of standard aligns with the purpose and philosophy of the group that creates the standards. Different interest groups who desire to promote their unique views or agenda through education can use different types of standards to achieve their goal.

There are different ways of organizing a response to the question of who makes the standards. National, state, and local groups can generate standards, or the question's answer can be

organized around the standards generated by professional education organizations, and private organizations. However the question is answered, one thing is certain, many individuals, groups, and organizations have input into the creation of educational standards.

National Standards

The idea of national standards implies that there are educational standards that are consistently used by all schools or universities in America. These could be mandated or voluntary, but in either case, the use of national standards implies a unified presentation of knowledge, skills, and attitudes in all educational institutions on a given level of matriculation, such as K-12, undergraduate, and graduate levels. Of course, national standards would only apply to public schools. Private schools, to some degree, may be affected by the public school standards, but their participation would be voluntary.

Some countries have education ministries, authorized by the national government, that organize their country's curriculum and instruction around national standards and have the authority to enforce the teaching and assessment of the standards. In the United States, the constitutional authority for public education is vested in the state governments. Nowhere in the constitution is authority over public education given to the federal government. However, in the United States, the federal government can greatly influence education through legislative mandates, such as the No Child Left Behind Act (NCLB), and through the allocation of federal funds to the states for educational purposes. In this case, if state and local schools desire the federal funds, they must comply with the conditions attached to the funding. This is an indirect way for the federal government to influence public education on a national level and, with the historical increase in federal education funding, a very effective method of influence. In relation to standards, the federal government cannot mandate national standards but can promote certain standards through the funding process.

Also, national standards can be promoted by other organizations. The *business sector* can lobby the federal government, state governments, local school boards, and individual educators to adopt standards that accommodate business interests. Through their well-established lobbying apparatus, their ability to use media to promote their ideas, and through the funding of educational programs, businesses can influence schools to adopt certain kinds of standards. Besides the business community, *professional educational organizations* and associations attempt to influence education through their promotion of educational standards. School districts, colleges, and universities on all levels can voluntarily agree to comply with accrediting agencies. This compliance requires the educational institution to agree to the standards created by the professional organization. Also, the scholarly community of the *universities* attempts to influence education on a national level. Through research and laboratory schools, universities attempt to develop curriculum, instruction, and assessment strategies and techniques that are promoted as educational "best practice." In the hope that this best practice will become the educational standard, they promote it through publication, as curriculum in higher education courses, and through university and school initiatives such as professional development schools. Through presentation and debate at national and regional educational conferences, educational scholars attempt to achieve a consensus of what constitutes best practice. Finally, *state governments* can attempt to promote national standards when state governors periodically meet.

Whether federal or state governments, the business sector, professional educational organizations, or universities, national standards can only be proposed not mandated. In this process of influencing education, the federal government has the most potential followed by professional organizations that offer national accreditation. However, many professional educational organizations primarily consist of university-affiliated individuals and are often sponsored by universities. Efforts to develop national standards by state governments depend upon the political influence that they have with the federal government.

State Standards

Within the last decade, most states have mandated some sort of standards-based curriculum for public schools on all educational levels. This trend has been accelerated by the federal mandates represented by the NCLB. Prior to the NCLB, the content and enforcement of state standards varied from state to state. Each state emphasized subject matter content that was deemed relevant

to their unique needs. In addition, each state independently determined to what degree local schools could have input into the construction of the standards and to what degree the standards would be enforced. Through the NCLB, the federal government now has greater influence in the promotion of standardized education in all states. This influence is seen not only in the reconstruction of state standards to accommodate NCLB mandates but also in the certification requirements for educators and in the accreditation process for colleges and universities. In most states, K-12 public schools are required to show evidence that they adhere to the state standards.

Local Standards

Historically, the power to set educational policy and standards has rested with the local school entity. Local schools were empowered by their state governments to set standards that best served the local interest. However, in the latter part of the twentieth century, this local autonomy has diminished with the growth of state and federal control. Issues involving economic prosperity and educational equity fostered this lessening of local control. Proponents of increased state and federal control have argued that local control created pockets of economically and socially disadvantaged individuals who suffered from conditions that could only be changed through external mandates. Prior to the increased federal and state mandates, parents, businesses, and other local interests experienced a greater degree of autonomy in setting educational standards.

Professional Organizations

There are a plethora of professional organizations that promote educational standards. These organizations represent specific subject areas, and fields of education. All of these organizations are comprised of a diversity of individuals ranging from educational researchers, educational practitioners, university scholars, business people, and politicians. Each organization promotes its own standards that represent the organization's perspective on best practice and the organization's political philosophy. Obviously, there is often no consensus between these various organizations in the standards that they promote. Some of these organizations have constructed and promoted standards relating to subject

matter and educational practice, while others promote educational policy that is to provide the philosophical and theoretical foundation for the construction of educational standards. Some organizations promote their standards by marketing textbooks and other educational materials that are based upon the standards that they developed.

The following is a list of some of the major professional organizations that have produced educational standards.

Subject-matter-focused professional organizations:
- International Reading Association
- National Council of Teachers of English
- National Council of Teachers of Mathematics
- National Council for the Social Studies
- National Science Board
- The American Association for the Advancement of Science
- The National Center for History in the Schools
- The Geography Education Standards Project
- National Council on Economic Education
- Center for Civic Education

Field-focused professional organizations:
- National Board for Professional Teaching Standards (NBPTS)
- Interstate New Teacher Assessment and Support Consortium (INTASC)
- National Council for the Accreditation of Teacher Education (NCATE)
- National Commission on Teaching and America's Future (NCTAF)
- Interstate School Leaders Licensure Consortium (ISLLC)
- Educational Leadership Constituent Council (ELCC)

The field-focused professional organizations are currently impacting public education by providing accreditation to colleges of education on the university level. Their standards affect all levels of education because to be accredited by these organizations requires a university to adopt and adhere to their standards for the training of preservice teachers, practicing teachers in advanced degree programs, and educational administrators and leaders who seek certification and advanced degrees. The standards pro-

moted by these organizations include subject matter and best practice instructional and management procedures.

Private Organizations

Private organizations, whether non-profit or for-profit, also participate in the construction of educational standards by either producing standards or by attempting to influence educational policy on all levels. Each of these organizations has a basic constituency and attempts to generate policy that supports the educational philosophy of their constituency. These organizations not only utilize national media to support their educational agendas but also provide funding for educational research. These organizations are aligned with specific political philosophies ranging from reactionary and conservative to liberal and radical. The following is a list of some of the more influential private organizations.

- Fordham Foundation
- Heritage Foundation
- Hudson Institute
- Olin Foundation
- The Pioneer Institute
- Manhattan Institute
- Brookings Institute
- The Century Foundation
- The Civil Rights Project at Harvard University
- National Education Association
- American Federation of Teachers

Who Should Make the Standards?

Possible answers to this question need to be framed within an understanding of the important effects that standards have on the lives of individuals who are held to the standards. When standards are accompanied by a high-stakes assessment, the potential effect on the individual greatly increases. States that use a high-stakes standardized test as the single indicator of student achievement of the standards establish conditions of success and failure that can change the direction of an individual's life. Failure to achieve an acceptable score on a test can lead to consequences such as not attaining a high school diploma, teacher certification,

or administrator certification or even dropping out of school. Other effects can include an educational experience of lesser quality and depth due to the endless repetition and rote memory that accompanies **teaching to the test.** The point is that standards and their accompanying assessment have the potential to seriously impact students. Therefore, determining who should make the standards and their assessment is a serious decision. An understanding of how this question may be answered involves a discussion of three aspects of who should make the standards: those individuals who are positioned within the great divides, the issue of relevance, and the psychometrician's view.

Teaching to the test

the singular use and prioritization of instructional strategies that are solely based on increasing student performance on a standardized test.

The Great Divides

The process of setting educational policy traditionally involves the contentious debate between groups that hold different positions on who should set educational policy—in this case, who should make the standards. These different positions can be essentialized into dichotomies that represent significant divisions regarding educational issues.

Practitioners or External Experts

The first divide is between those who think that educational practitioners should make this decision and those who advocate external experts as the decision makers. Proponents of the practitioner as decision maker represent the thinking that those who are closest to the students and the educational environment should be the major decision makers. They argue that teachers, administrators, and parents, who are the stakeholders closest to the learning process, should determine the standards and their assessment strategy. Schools that adhere to this view form panels of teachers, administrators, parents, and curriculum specialists, who then construct the standards and the assessments. They maintain that the uniqueness of the local environment is then included in the process as a mediating factor that ensures educational relevance and authenticity. Factors in the local environment that are addressed in the standard-making process range from social, cultural, historical and economic conditions characteristic of the local area, to the socioeconomic status of the community and the cultural capital brought to the learning process by the students. Conversely, they argue that national or regional standards

developed by external authorities cannot account for the impact of the local uniqueness on the educational process. Therefore, externally imposed standards are artificial constructions that provide little benefit for the students and the local community in which they live.

In opposition to this opinion is the view that external experts who hold a more formal and authoritative understanding of the content, skills, and attitudes that will be represented by the standards should make the standards and assessments. In addition, proponents of this view argue that these experts have the capacity to see the larger national, state, or regional context that is to be served by student attainment of the standards. Those in the federal government and the states that adhere to this view form panels that consist of business CEOs, politicians, government officials, representatives of government think tanks, and representatives of ideological think tanks. Also included may be university experts and a scattering of educational practitioners. Since the harsh criticism of public education that began in the 1980s, many of the national and state government panels that established standards-related policy have predominately consisted of noneducational experts. Within this view is the promotion of national, state, or regional interests over those of the local communities. Local uniqueness and its expression in the local control of education are not only considered irrelevant to the construction of standards but also seen as a potential source of inefficient and inequitable education. Those who support the authority of external experts argue that the interests of all individuals are best served through a standardized curriculum and that local compliance can only be obtained through the assessment of the standards with a stringent standardized assessment that guarantees local accountability to the standards.

Theory or Practice

Another divide that is related to the division between practitioners and external experts is that between theory and practice. Traditionally, in their decision-making, educational practitioners rely upon their grounding in educational theory initially obtained in their degree work, their field experience, and their professional intuition. The constraints of the workplace allow little time for educators to engage theory. Educational theory only becomes

part of the practitioner's experience through isolated professional development opportunities and from some courses taken for advanced degrees. Experts in the field of education who have little or no contact with the school environment base their decisions on their formative educational experience and primarily on theory that is generated through educational research. Non-educational experts base their decisions about education on the theory, practice, and experience related to their own field. For instance, business leaders who are involved in educational policy decisions rely upon the research-based best practices and theories of their field to make decisions about education. Therefore, there is a divide over what constitutes best practice between educational practitioners, educational scholars, and non-educators. One consequence of this divide in educational decision making is that either the positive experiences of the practitioner, the theory of the educational scholars, or the relevant theory and practice of non-educational experts may be excluded from the policy-making process. Also, the theory and practice of others may be included only in an instrumental and selective manner to accommodate the primary decision-makers' own perspective. In this case, the intrinsically valuable information and experiences of those who are left out of the process that can enhance the quality of the standards and their assessment are lost in the process.

Centralized or decentralized education

This division involves the debate concerning the **centralization** or **decentralization** of education. Proponents of the centralization of education propose that education needs to be nationally standardized in order to promote a common culture based upon common core knowledge and common values (Gaddy, Hall, & Marzano, 1996; Schlesinger, 1998; U.S. Department of Education, 2001). Decentralists argue that a centralized educational system will devalue the diversity and difference that naturally occurs in society. Decentralists see national standards and standardized testing as mechanisms that promote the melting pot theory of society that is in opposition to the growing multiculturalism of the United States (Giroux, 1996; Kincheloe & Steinberg, 1997; Spring, 2001). Of course, the important issue in this debate is who establishes the national standards. Either side in this divisive debate recognizes that all standards and assessments

Centralized education
education that is controlled and standardized by a central authority such as the national government.

Decentralized education
all aspects of education are controlled by local communities.

represent specific values. Therefore, who makes the standards also sets the values that will be taught through the standards.

Intellectualism Versus Anti-Intellectualism

The divide between university scholars and practitioners is further accentuated by the anti-intellectualism that has historically permeated American society. (Hofstadter, 1964). At various times, intellectualism has been denigrated and viewed as irrelevant to the practical matters of society. In opposition to intellectualism is the philosophy of rugged individualism that relies upon individual knowledge gained primarily through experience. This reaction to intellectualism is most often represented in the categorization of scholars as residents of the "ivory tower." As educational practitioners struggle with the exigencies of their workplace experiences, they tend to discount the theory proposed by intellectuals that is disconnected from their real life experience and rely upon their own situational and pragmatic solutions. This division between theory and practice is evident in the resistance of practitioners and some members of the general public to standards and assessment strategies that are primarily theoretical and not a part of their personal and professional experience (such as standards of complexity, authentic assessment, and portfolio assessment). Conversely, practitioners and the general public may more readily accept standards and assessment strategies that are grounded less in research-based best practice and more in their own lived experience as students and teachers.

The Relevance of Standards

All those who participate in the construction of educational standards are concerned about the relevance of the standards. However, the essential question related to relevance is: To whom are standards relevant? This is an essential question because of the central role that education plays in reproducing the knowledge, skills, and attitudes that constitute American society. Therefore, what is taught in schools is of central importance—of great relevance—to any individuals or groups who want their ideas firmly entrenched in American culture. One way to create the potential for the entrenchment of their ideas is to ensure that educational standards represent what they consider to be appropriate knowl-

edge, skills, and attitudes. Therefore, different types of standards are related to the different views of individuals and groups.

To Whom Are Standards Relevant?

Should standards be relevant to the needs of the student, the business sector, or government officials? How this question is answered directly impacts the type of standards that will be constructed. If standards are constructed to meet any of the groups identified in the question or to accommodate all of these groups, they will be inherently different.

For instance, *student-centered standards* will accommodate the diverse needs of students and consequently provide them with the knowledge, skills, and attitudes that will enable them to lead socially rich and productive lives within a rapidly changing information society. These standards would include a basic knowledge base in all subjects that would be posed in an interdisciplinary context that recognizes the interconnectedness of knowledge and the fact that knowledge changes at a rapid pace. Proponents of interdisciplinary standards argue that these are important because in their lives students seldom encounter situations in which one type of subject matter is isolated from the others. They believe that the problems and situations that individuals encounter require an interrelated command of the knowledge and skills of many subjects that mediate and inform each other. Therefore, to properly prepare students to deal with situations by utilizing knowledge and skills from different disciplines in a holistic manner is the essence of authentic and relevant education. They further believe that because students live in an increasingly pluralistic society, included within the knowledge base that they learn would be the formal knowledge of the disciplines and the indigenous knowledge of the subcultures and groups that comprise our pluralistic society.

Critical thinking skills, such as analysis, synthesis, and evaluation, would be included in the standards. The standards would require the students to utilize these skills to interrogate the knowledge that they acquire, the consequences of acting on that knowledge, and the historical foundations of that knowledge. Since power arrangements permeate our democratic society, the standards would require students to use their critical thinking skills in a critical investigation of these power arrangements and

of the consequences of the use of power in relation to the issues of social justice, an ethic of caring, and democratic participation.

In student-centered standards, because the learning of the knowledge and skills that are a part of student-centered standards closely approximates real-life experiences, the assessment of these standards would be multiple and authentic. Because of their focus on only certain aspects of a knowledge base or specific skills, single assessment instruments are believed to have great difficulty in capturing the holistic nature of real-life experiences. Therefore, proponents argue that multiple assessments of various kinds must be utilized to evaluate all of the aspects of the learning experience. Because the student is the focus of the assessment, the multiple assessments would be both formative (diagnostic) and summative (evaluative) in nature.

Standards that are relevant to the needs of the business sector would require all students to acquire basic knowledge, skills, and attitudes related to the students' future roles as consumers, workers, and generally as participants within a market economy. As previously mentioned in a *business-centered standards* environment, knowledge and skills would be prioritized with the higher priority assigned to the knowledge and skills necessary for entry into the workforce. Reading, writing, math, and science would take precedence over the social sciences and fine arts. One purpose of the assessment of standards would be to rank and sort workers in relation to their future occupational and vocational levels. Students' achievement of the standards would determine their transition to different preparation tracks leading to different vocations and levels within the vocations. Standardized assessments would be the most efficient type of measurements because of their ability to rank and sort students in relation to their attainment of the standards. Standardized assessments would also function as diagnostic tools that would indicate which students would enter remediation loops within the prioritized content areas and which would move on to different content areas and different levels within the content areas. Factory-style instructional systems would be constructed to accommodate business-centered standards. These standards would be more behavioralistic and reductionist in that they would focus on specific, isolated facts and skills separate from the holistic context in which they naturally occur. Proponents of business-centered standards argue that

by reducing a complex whole to its decontextualized parts, student attainment of these bits of knowledge and skill can be more efficiently assessed.

Government-centered standards would be constructed to accommodate national security needs and the needs of those groups who have influence with the government officials. The government reaction to the *Sputnik* crisis in the late 1950s, and the government reaction to the deteriorating economy of the 1970s and 1980s are examples of this view on standards. In the former example, the federal government, influenced by military-driven security needs, stressed academic standards in math and science, and in the latter, they stressed business-centered standards, due to the influence of the business community. Since government is inherently political, the standards proposed by the government would be in response to the political ideologies that control the government, and the special interest groups that influence elected government officials. Government-centered standards could be focused on citizenship. However, citizenship is politically defined in many ways, and this variance in definition would reflect the socially dominant group's definition.

As previously discussed, standards are relevant also to the interests of other groups such as institutions of higher education, local communities, and society in general. Like student-centered, business-centered, and government-centered standards, these other interests would also want standards to be constructed that specifically reflect their own agendas. Many of these other groups lobby for standards that are essentially *ideology-driven standards.* In this case, an individual's position on the political spectrum defines which types of standards are considered relevant. Reactionaries, conservatives, moderates, liberals, and radicals all hold distinctly different views of what constitutes valid and appropriate standards. Through the years, educational policy has been variously affected by conservative, liberal, and radical views. Conservative thought dominated educational policy in the 1950s and from the 1980s to the present. During the 1920s, 1930s, and the 1960s liberal views influenced education. Radical views on education have always been on the periphery of educational policy and practice. The point is that the knowledge, skills, and attitudes represented in educational standards of various time periods have always reflected the dominant political philosophy of that time

period. The type of educational standard that is promoted at a given time is directly related to the dominant political philosophy of that time. One recurring phenomenon that reflects the political influence on educational standards is the ongoing battle between the proponents of a common culture and those of a pluralistic culture. Some scholars argue that the current standards and accountability initiative, as best exemplified by NCLB, is the latest attempt to promote a common white Eurocentric culture at a time when America is demographically becoming a multicultural society. Subsequently, they further argue that the standards promoted by this initiative promote the type of knowledge, skills, and attitudes that will sustain the dominant white and Eurocentric culture. These different ideological groups attempt to influence education in the hopes of promoting their agendas. These groups seek to codify in standards the knowledge, skills, and attitudes that serve their interests. Conservatives and liberals attempt to establish their views and values in public school students by having students learn the standards that represent their particular view. Business groups attempt to pass along their training costs to public schools. Also, different social classes and cultural groups attempt to reproduce in public school students the knowledge and values that ensure a continuation of their way of life and their dominance of American society. In these cases, through the manipulation of educational standards supported by rigorous accountability systems, these groups view education, and subsequently the students, as means to their ends.

The Psychometrician's View of Who Should Make Standards

One position on who should make the standards that are generally identified by others proposes that psychometricians should construct the standards. Psychometric psychologists are experts who deal with the use of statistical methods to measure mental development. This field attempts to provide a reasoned and objective method to determine who should make the standards and how valid and reliable standards can be constructed. The field of psychometrics is primarily involved in the development of standardized tests in education. Advanced statistical analysis is used to determine if a test is valid, meaning that it measures what it purports to measure, and whether it is reliable, meaning that the test is consistently valid in relation to individual and geographical differences. Tests such as the SAT and the NAEP are constantly statistically scrutinized in order to eliminate any biases that could invalidate the test for specific individuals and groups. One aspect of this search for validity involves the relationship between the standards and the instrument used in their assessment. Before a test can be proven to be valid, it must show internal validity. Internal validity measures whether the assessment instrument, the test, is aligned with the standards. In other words, does the test actually measure the standards, or are there other variables that skew the test results. Because of this concern for internal validity, how the standards are constructed is an important psychometric issue.

Since the defensibility of the standards is crucial in establishing validity, psychometricians propose reasonable and systematic processes in the creation of the standards (Cizek, 2001). Because standards are usually constructed by a group of individuals, the panel, and the selection process and training of the panel are of utmost importance. To allay concerns about bias, psychometricians suggest that the panels should be large and representative of the stakeholders who will be affected by the standards. Some psychometric models propose that to provide the needed diversity attention must be given to the geographical, cultural, gender, age, technical background, and educational responsibilities of the panelists (Hambleton, 2001; Jaeger, 1991). To ensure this degree of diversity, a second sample of panelists is selected to go through the same standards-setting process as the first, and the resultant standards of the two groups should coincide. Instead of using commercial testing organizations, some states such as New York use their own state and local officials to construct, field test, publish, and score their state exams (Hoff, 2003). In the field of psychometrics, there are variations on the selection of panels and the reliability of the resultant standards, but all of these processes seek to provide a panel that accurately represents the diversity of the group that will be affected by the standards.

Once the panel(s) is established, training of the panelists ensues. In this training, the panelists learn how to perform two very important initial tasks. First, they must acquire an understanding of the context of the standard-setting activity and the

environment to which the standard will be applied. Second, they must develop an operational definition of borderline examinee performance on the assessment instrument that will measure student attainment of the standards. In addition, panelists must understand the purpose of the exam, the rationale for and consequences of the standard setting, the characteristics of the examinee population, the education and training experiences of the examinee population, and the psychological factors related to learning and academic achievement. Also, they must have a detailed knowledge of the subject that is being assessed, the characteristics of the test questions that can influence the difficulty that an examinee will encounter in answering the questions correctly, and the characteristics of the examinee that will also influence the difficulty of the questions (Raymond & Reid, 2001).

Psychometricians emphasize the importance of the selection process of the participants who will serve on the panel. They caution that how well the panel represents the affected stakeholder group and the qualifications of the panel participants not only affects the validity of the standards but also how the standards and assessment are perceived by various communities of interest (Raymond & Reid, 2001). These psychometric concerns are well taken; however, as previously discussed, the making of standards is an inherently political process in that the type of standards that are made represents values that will coincide with a specific purpose or philosophy. The political context of standard making and its subsequent political consequences may offset even the best efforts to ensure statistical objectivity (Popham, 2001; Raymond & Reid, 2001). If a group that represents a specific political, economic, cultural, or social position has control over the selection and training of the panel participants, they can meet the geographical, cultural, gender, age, technical background, and educational requirements posed by the psychometricians but do so with individuals who are in agreement with the specific view that is to be promoted in the standards and the assessment. Therefore, within the guise of objectivity, the subjective view of one group representing one purpose or philosophy can make standards that promote their view. In the end, those who select the panel also indirectly make the standards.

The Many Types of Standards

In a very general way all standards are expectations of teaching and learning. However, the term "expectations" can be defined in numerous ways. The general public usually only hears the generic term, "standards"; however, within the educational community practitioners are fast becoming acquainted with a diversity of terms that actually represent distinctly different types of standards and the related different purposes and philosophies that are behind each type. The following section is a brief explanation of the more common types of standards.

National Standards

At this time, there are no national standards in the United States; however, there is a growing lobby that supports the institution of standards that would be mandated for all schools. The term "national standards" implies that a national curriculum would be established that would define the knowledge, skills, and attitudes that would be consistently taught in all schools. Proponents of national standards also propose that a series of standardized tests would be used to assess student achievement of these standards. At this time the NAEP test is mandated by the national government and are used to assess the effectiveness of student learning in certain content areas across the United States. Test data is used to measure individual student learning and the variance of this learning in American states and communities. Since there is no formal national curriculum upon which the test is based, the test content acts as an ad hoc curriculum.

State Standards

This term applies to the educational standards independently established by each state. Since the individual states hold the legal responsibility for education, each state has the power to set its own standards. Currently, the NCLB Act and the NAEP test are shaping state standards. Through legislation and the conditional provision of federal funds, the federal government is influencing state standards and attempting to promote a nationwide curricular continuity. State standards are established for all public educational institutions, whether K-12 or higher education. State standards can be viewed on the website of each state's Department of Education.

Content Standards

Even though this type of standard measures the content of a specific subject area, content standards can range from broad conceptual statements referring to student understanding of some aspect of the targeted content to specific facts that students will memorize and recall. An example of a broad or conceptual content standard would be Theme VI (f.) from the Curriculum Standards for Social Studies (National Council for the Social Studies, 1994): "Analyze and evaluate conditions, actions, and motivations that contribute to conflict and cooperation within and among nations." In contrast, a more factually oriented content standard is Standard 4A, 7–12, ERA 6 of the National Standards for History (National Center for History in the Schools, 1996): "Explain the provisions of the Dawes Severalty Act of 1887 and evaluate its effects on tribal identity, land ownership, and assimilation." Many state history content standards are even more reductionist in that they are very directive in the requirement of students to recall specific lists of individuals, events, and other historical information. Generally, content standards developed by professional organizations tend to be more conceptual than factual, with state standards being more factual than conceptual. The more factual content standards better lend themselves to assessment by objective standardized tests and also more effectively control an individual teacher's ability to manipulate the content and assessment of the content.

Content standards are also political in that what content is included or excluded in standards represents the different ideological interpretations of the subject area. In the late 1980s, E. D. Hirsch, Jr. (1988; Hirsch, Jr., Kett, & Trefil, 1988) promoted a specific curriculum that defined "what every American needs to know." This curriculum has been widely criticized by liberals and radicals as specifically representing only the knowledge that will reproduce a culturally conservative view in students. The knowledge that is included and excluded from content standards, the implied correct interpretation of that knowledge, what students are asked to do with that knowledge, and how that knowledge is assessed, are mediated and informed by the political context of the individuals who construct the content standards. In this case, the politically mandated knowledge identified by

those in control of society gains value as the cultural capital that is required for individuals to have success in school and eventually in the larger society.

Outcome or Performance Standards

Some individuals who construct standards envision content standards as only the starting point. They maintain that content standards need performance descriptions of what students need to do to show their mastery of the content standard. The addition of performance criteria transforms the content standard into outcome or performance standards. Performance criteria are specific descriptors of what students need to do to show mastery. These criteria often utilizes the terminology found in Bloom's (Bloom, Englelhart, Furst, Hill, & Krathwhol, 1956) taxonomy of educational objectives. Students may be instructed to list, compare, analyze, synthesize, and evaluate. Other instructions may direct the student to draw, write, recite, or graph the information. However, the key component of all performance standards is the very specific instructions that regulate the students' responses. Tucker and Codding (1998) describe good standards (performance standards) as those standards that include three components: a performance description as a narrative statement of what students must know and do, samples of student work that personify correct mastery of the standard, and commentaries on the student work that identify features of the student work that comply with the standard. Often rubrics, or scoring guides, are developed to provide the evaluative criteria that enable evaluators to determine the extent to which students have demonstrated mastery of the performance standard and to determine different levels of achievement among the students.

Outcome or performance standards are the center of what is known as **standards-based education** and standards-based or referenced assessment. In standards-based education and standards-based assessment, the whole educational system is focused on the performance standards. The mission of the school is driven by student achievement of the performance standards. In an ideal form, the education and assessment of students are focused on the performance of individual students. These students are not to be normatively compared with other students or to a national average. However, one of the frequent byproducts

Standards-based education

all aspects of an educational environment are focused on a set of guiding standards.

of this type of system is the ease with which students, teachers, schools, and communities can be ranked and sorted in relation to their effectiveness in meeting the standards. In this case, standards-based learning places the primary focus for learning on individuals. Some argue that this individualistic focus allows system-wide economic, political, cultural, and social phenomena, such as educational funding, racism, sexism, classism, etc., to be ignored.

Some individuals such as Sandra Wilde (2002) caution that even though performance standards provide "intelligent assessment, improve accountability, and provide direction for future instruction" (p. 81), they have the greatest potential for abuse. Wilde identifies this potential for abuse as occurring when individual student differences are not taken into account during the assessment process. Wilde points out that when narrow assessment tools such as standardized tests with inappropriately high stakes are used, the positive attributes of performance standards are distorted. In addition, others argue that negative educational outcomes can occur when performance standards are rigidly enforced, are the primary means to organize student inquiry into knowledge, and are the only criteria used to measure student learning. Their position is that the sole reliance on this type of standard can negatively affect teacher judgment in curriculum determination, student activity, and assessment of student progress.

Grade-Level Standards

Grade-level standards are established for specific grades and act as indicators of student mastery of the performance standards for a specific grade. Due to NCLB pressure and their own choosing, states are establishing grade-level standards that are used in a high-stakes context to determine whether a student is allowed to pass to the next grade level. Some states establish standardized tests at specific grades, such as third, fifth, eighth, tenth, and twelfth, to measure student attainment of the performance standards. These tests become high-stakes exit-level tests if the students are required to pass the test before moving to the next grade level or receiving a high school diploma. Higher education also utilizes a form of the grade-level standards concept if students are required to show proficiency in the mastering of performance standards before entering an area of certification or before receiving a professional certification. On the other end of the educational spectrum, 39 states and the District of Columbia have crafted or are developing standards for preschool children (Jacobson, 2003). Some proponents of preschool standards propose academic standards that relate to the tests that students will begin taking in early childhood. Others argue that because research shows that social and emotional development affect later school performance, physical, social, and emotional standards need to be emphasized (Jacobson, 2003).

Grade-level standards may be diagnostic in nature rather than high stakes. Some schools are establishing pre-kindergarten performance standards for the purpose of making judgments about student readiness in relation to a later high-stakes test in grades two or three. Student achievement of these standards can be used to determine remediation loops or to track students into homogeneous grade levels or tracks. As in content and performance standards, grade-level standards send specific messages about what knowledge is valued and about the effectiveness of individual students, teachers, and schools in relation to the values of those who established the grade-level standards.

Functional Standards

Some educators (Resnick & Nolan, 1995) distinguish between functional standards and other types of standards that are less directive as to what knowledge is to be learned and the specificity regarding the process of learning the knowledge. Resnick and Nolan's view of functional standards is typical in that the basic components include content standards, performance standards, "good-enough" criteria, benchmark examples of student work, and benchmark commentary.

Besides the desired specificity found in performance standards, *benchmarking* is a critical ingredient of functional standards. Benchmarks represent best practices or critical knowledge that are found through a search of educational research or through an analysis of what other selected countries are doing in relation to knowledge and skills (Tucker & Codding, 1998). The basic assumption behind benchmarking is that our content and performance standards need to function in relation to consensual best practice or selected global educational practices. The aspect of the current standards movement in the United States that focuses on

global educational competition places great value on European and Asian educational organization and practices such as national curriculum, performance standards, and standardized testing. In this view, what students learn and how they learn in other countries become the benchmarks for American education. Therefore the functional goal of American education is to be competitive with these other countries by emulating their educational structures and practices. The term *World Class* standards is derived from this process of benchmarking (Bush, 1991). American standards, which are proposed as World Class standards, are thought to be equivalent in quality to those European and Asian standards that are the reason why their students allegedly outperform American students. The idea of World Class standards is rooted in the assumption that economic productivity is related to specific educational content, instruction, and organization. In the Clinton administration's Goals 2000 initiative, the term World Class standards became simply *World Standards;* however, the intent remained the same.

Opportunity-to-Learn Standards

Opportunity-to-learn standards (OTL), a part of the Goals 2000 initiative, are standards that focus on the resources, practices, and conditions that are necessary for all students to learn in an equitable way. Highly controversial, OTL has yet to be implemented in a comprehensive way as a national standards strategy; however, aspects of OTL are evident in NCLB. The controversy revolves around which variables that affect student learning should be part of OTL. As summarized by Andrew C. Porter (1995), OTL standards could include "availability to students of good curricula, instructional materials, and technologies; teachers capable of providing high-quality instruction; educators with access to professional development; safe and secure school facilities; and school policies that ensure nondiscrimination. In addition, curriculum, instructional practices, and assessments were to be consistent with voluntary national content standards" (p. 53). Much of what Porter wrote about has become part of NCLB. However, one important aspect of equitable education that has not been addressed and fuels the controversy is equitable educational funding. OTL standards are focused on individual students, educators, and school, and tend to not address the economic,

political, cultural, and social variables that also affect the issue of equitable student learning. One criticism of narrowly focused OTL standards is that they ignore these aspects of the larger society in which schools and educational stakeholders are nested (Natriello, 1996).

OTL standards attempt to address the equity concerns that have arisen from the use of high-stakes standardized tests. Some argue that if students are to be ranked and sorted through a standardized test, then they should all have an equal playing field (Noddings, 1997). One issue surrounding OTL standards is that of who should ensure this equal playing field. Some critics of OTL see this movement as another federal intrusion into state and local education. Others who agree with OTL maintain that the federal government is responsible for the funding that will guarantee equitable education for all students. Another issue relates to the fact that OTL is based exclusively upon one philosophy of standards, as exemplified by performance standards, at the expense of other standards philosophies. In other words, an OTL mandate would require all schools to comply with this curriculum, instruction, and assessment view of education. While the OTL movement recognizes the issue of educational equity, it is mired in the politics of education.

New Standards

The New Standards represent the efforts by the National Center on Education and the Economy, and the Learning Research and Development Center at the University of Pittsburgh to develop a performance and assessment system for elementary, middle, and high school students (New Standards, n.d.). New Standards provides internationally benchmarked performance standards for English and language arts, mathematics, science, and applied learning. These standards are derived from the national content standards developed by a coalition of professional organizations such as the National Council of Teachers of Mathematics, the American Association for the Advancement of Science, The National Council of Teachers of English, and the University of California.

New Standards exceeds the federal effort, NCLB, to establish performance standards in that they promote a more extensive

system-wide change effort, the idea of a "quality triangle," and reference examinations. New Standards is a system-wide change effort because it goes beyond just setting standards and requiring a standardized test to include most of the components of a school system, such as the curriculum framework, instruction, instructional materials, school organization, school management, and teacher training. All of these systemic components are centered upon the performance standards and the reference examinations. Some schools that use the New Standards, because of the pressure of the NCLB mandate, employ the strategy of teaching to the standardized test that makes them accountable for student achievement. However, the New Standards utilize the whole educational environment to promote student learning of the performance standards.

New Standards also differ from the federal standards and accountability initiative by envisioning the learning process as a quality triangle. These three essential parts focus on course content expressed as performance standards or only those things that can be assessed, the use of actual student work or products that meet the performance standards, and the use of the standards to guide the learning processes used by the students (Tucker & Codding, 1998).

Also, unlike many state performance assessments that are influenced by the NCLB requirements, the New Standards examinations are tightly referenced to or aligned with the performance standards. Indeed, through the use of what they call reference examinations, the New Standards strive to align the written, taught, and tested curriculum.

One criticism of the New Standards from content specialists is that, in relation to content, they are reductionistic in that not all of the content in each targeted discipline is taught. Proponents of the New Standards recognize this criticism and point out that first, there is not enough time in the school day or year to teach all of the content in each discipline and that the mastery of essential concepts takes precedence over facts that are unrelated to real-world problems (Tucker & Codding, 1998). Other critics of this reduction in content focus not so much on the fact that not everything can be taught but rather over *who* determines what content will be taught. Those individuals who constructed the New Standards made this decision by first engaging in the international benchmarking process. Educational experts in European and Asian countries who were determined to be educationally successful were questioned as to what they taught and how they taught.

Another criticism of the New Standards is that they are primarily focused on the promotion of content and skills that directly relate to success in the workforce and increased economic productivity. In a criticism of this focus on types of worker characteristics that is represented in the New Standards and similar economically based standards, Henry M. Levin (2001) makes two points. First, he points out that worker characteristics identified by standards are based upon knowledge; however, most desired worker characteristics encompass behaviors and habits such as teamwork, collaboration, initiative, and forms of problem solving that require adaptability and spontaneous responses (Levin, 2001, p. 47). Levin accurately points out that these characteristics are not measured on existing standardized test instruments. He also states that there is little research validation of the claim that economic productivity and knowledge-focused teaching are connected. In addition, Robert L. Linn (1996) argues that there is no empirical evidence that the new standardized high-stakes tests that are being used are more predictive of worker productivity than traditional measures.

High Standards

A much-used term in the standards and accountability movement is that of high standards. This is an ambiguous term that is widely used by a diversity of individuals to indicate a difference between standards that are more rigorous than others. The definition of high standards is relative to the way that one defines rigor. Different educational fields, ideologies, and special interests may construct very different definitions of what constitutes a rigorous or high standard. Understanding how different views of curriculum, instruction and assessment inform the different definitions of high standards greatly facilitates the ability to distinguish between the different definitions and, more importantly, their consequences.

Power Standards

Within an educational leadership context, Douglas B. Reeves (2002) proposes power standards. Reeves' development of this view on standards is an excellent example of the dilemma that faces many administrators and teachers who are in a standardized testing accountability situation. In this situation, Reeves sees only two choices: either engage in an increasingly superficial coverage of the mandated curriculum or add value to the state standards through a process of prioritization. The result of this prioritization process is an identification of the standards that are more important than others. These more important standards become the power standards. The criteria that Reeves uses to identify power standards are endurance, leverage, and readiness for the next level of instruction. Standards that endure are those skills and knowledge that remain with students long after the completion of the standardized test. Leverage refers to standards that apply to many academic disciplines. Standards that comply with the readiness for the next level of learning criteria are those that prepare a student for success in the next grade level. Reeves argues that these criteria allow the identification of the standards that are the most valuable to students and the schools. However, Reeves does caution that the potential danger in the use of power standards is that those standards that do not become power standards may well appear as questions on the test. Power standards are a reflection of the debate over 100% coverage and partial mastery of mandated standards or less coverage and full mastery of some standards.

Maverick Standards

The term maverick standards has been coined by Deborah Meier (2000) to distinguish between standards established by individual schools and educators that do not comply with more established or mandated types of standards. Through the use of this term, Meier argues that these locally constructed standards can be high standards in their academic rigor, and also authentically relevant to the local context in which they were constructed and are employed. Meier suggests that when standards are constructed by those closest to the local context, they can more fully meet the specific needs of the students and the local edu-

cational environment than externally imposed decontextualized standards.

Professional Standards

This category of standards constitutes all of the standards developed by professional organizations. The targets of these standards are the colleges and universities that certify teachers and educational leaders. Adherence to these standards is voluntary, and compliance with the standards is rewarded with a designated accreditation status. Accreditation occurs after a visiting team from the accrediting organization certifies university compliance with the organization's standards. The purpose of this effort to accredit institutions of higher learning is to promote a greater degree of professionalism, a higher quality education, and an organizational and curricular continuity among the various colleges and universities. The main advantage in attaining accreditation involves the increase in status of the university that then allegedly can be used in the attraction of students to the university's programs. Institutions of higher learning expend significant time and financial resources in complying with the accreditation process and in the achievement of accredited status. One main evaluative focus of accrediting bodies is the content and organization of the curriculum. The bias of the accrediting agency can shape the university's curriculum. For instance, if the agency does not value foundational courses such as history and philosophy, the accreditation process can be structured to achieve this goal (Creighton & Young, 2003). Other accreditation concerns deal with non-curriculum conditions such as the ratios of tenure track professors to the use of adjunct and non-tenure track professors. In some cases, universities must increase the number of tenure track professors to meet the professional standard, thus adding to the university's cost in faculty salary.

Professional standards of this sort are part of an internal initiative by universities to enhance the level of professionalism in the field of education. State mandates supercede all professional standards. Adherence to professional accreditation standards does not allow colleges of education to certify educators. Only the state in which the university resides can grant educational institutions the right to certify educators. The accreditation movement

started in the 1990s as an educational response to the criticisms of education that began in the early 1980s. Examples of comprehensive accrediting organizations that evaluate all organizational and curricular aspects of an institution would include National Council for Accreditation of Teacher Education, Interstate School Leaders Licensure Consortium and Interstate New Teacher Assessment and Support Consortium.

K-12 public schools can also participate in the accreditation process. Regional professional organizations exist that provide this service. Once again, this is a voluntary process since all public schools answer to their states. All states have their own procedures that assess the individual schools 'compliance with the state' standards.

Two Essential Categories of Standards: Technical Standards and Standards of Complexity

Understanding the current standards and accountability phenomenon requires a concomitant understanding of the philosophical foundations of two essentially different views on the nature, purpose, and function of standards. All of the different types of standards fall within two essential categories: technical standards and standards of complexity. Each category has very different consequences and implications for educational practice and all educational stakeholders. The essential difference in the nature of these two categories is seen in how each defines curriculum, instruction, and assessment. Each of these components of both categories is tightly aligned with a basic philosophy that provides the foundation for the category. Both technical standards and standards of complexity represent historically different philosophies or views on the nature of knowledge, how knowledge is acquired, and how the acquisition of knowledge is assessed.

The Philosophical Foundation of Technical Standards

Technical standards are grounded in the realism and scientific rationality of Western Europe that arose in the Age of Enlightenment. Realists believe that there is an objective and quantifiable reality that is external to human consciousness. This reality can be discovered and empirically verified by experts who are trained to employ scientific procedures, objective measurement, and statistical analysis. In addition, the use of scientific rationality guarantees the certainty of the conclusions that are drawn about the natural world and human activity. Certainty is also achieved by identifying patterns of cause and effect that can be determined by isolating and controlling variables through statistical analysis and scientific procedures. One result of this rational process is a view of reality that separates phenomenon into binaries. Because of the perceived certainty of the discovered knowledge, the natural world and human activity can be classified into simple, definitive binary structures such as science and superstition, civilized and uncivilized, good and bad, modern and backward, correct and incorrect, valid and invalid, male and female, effective and ineffective, Caucasian and non-white, and so forth. One outcome of this dualistic view is that the inherent complexity found in nature and in human activity is lost. Based upon their scientifically grounded certainty, realists are positive that their dualistic categorization of nature and human activity is an accurate representation of reality.

In many ways realism has been the dominant philosophy during the age of modernism. Modernistic society is characterized as essentially an industrial-age society that values stability, certainty, and Western European values. Through the Industrial Revolution to the present, modernistic thinking has used scientific rationality as the foundational method of inquiry to determine the basic assumptions about how things work and why things are a certain way. Modernists are positivists in that they are certain—positive—about the nature of reality because of their belief in the reliability of scientific procedures to discover the objective natural laws that govern reality.

In relation to education, technical standards are philosophically grounded in the realist, positivist thinking of the modern age. As earlier discussed, the scientific management of education, the Social Efficiency Movement, and the adoption of business practices in education are modernistic views about the nature of teaching and learning. All of these modernistic views regard curriculum, teaching, and assessment as activities that can be scientifically managed with certainty and predictability. Because knowledge is independent of human consciousness and can be discovered and quantified, curriculum exists as an entity that is independent from the student. In modernistic educational thinking, curriculum is subject based with the subjects arranged in a hierarchy of importance. Since knowledge is gained through sci-

entific rationality, subjects such as math, science, reading and writing have precedence over others because they provide the essential tools for the discovery of knowledge. In relation to teaching, those who have acquired the discovered knowledge can transmit the curriculum to the students. The role of the teacher is to facilitate the development of rational thought processes in the students so that they can eventually also discover the knowledge found in the basic laws of nature. In addition, teachers are sources of authority who can determine correct and incorrect answers that students provide or simply transmit the correct information to the students. Paolo Freire (1985, 1996) described this modernistic method of instruction as the banking method of instruction. In this method, the expert or teacher deposits information into the minds of passive students. Modernists also believe that instructional effectiveness and efficiency can be achieved by reducing teaching to discrete parts that can be scientifically managed. Likewise, assessment becomes a simple act of determining whether the students correctly learned the required knowledge. Effective and efficient assessment is that which lends itself to the statistical analysis of student learning. Standardized assessment is appropriate because all students must learn the objective knowledge that has been scientifically discovered. Since students do not construct their own knowledge, students can be efficiently ranked and sorted by their ability to learn the predetermined knowledge.

In modernistic educational environments, every aspect of the educational process can be controlled; every task can be standardized; detailed statistical records identify student learning; every stakeholder has a specialized role; curriculum and instruction can be precisely determined and executed, and standardized assessment guarantees accountability to the curricular and instructional decisions of the content experts. In addition, statistical analysis and scientific procedures can uncover cause-and-effect relationships that can be generalized to all educational settings. Dualistic decisions can be made about good and bad or effective and ineffective curriculum, instruction, assessment, teachers, and students.

The Philosophical Foundation
of Standards of Complexity

Standards of complexity are grounded in the postpositivist thinking of the twentieth century and in American pragmatism that is best represented by the work of John Dewey. During the twentieth century, the positivist view of modernistic reality increasingly came under attack from various individuals who collectively can be referred to as postpositivists. Postpositivist thinkers represent a shared critique of the realistic philosophy of positivism and the certainty of the causal relations that are promoted by scientific rationality. Postpositivist thinking in the form of poststructuralism (Palmer, 1997), postmodernism (Grenz, 1996; Powell, 1998), and critical theory constructed new interpretations of human activity in relation to the social, cultural, and physical environment.

To some degree, all postpositivist thinking is part of the philosophical foundation of standards of complexity. For instance, poststructural and postmodern analysis problematized the foundations of modernist thinking by uncovering the inconsistencies and value-laden assumptions upon which modernistic thought and activity are based. After World War II, existentialist philosophy promoted a subjective view of reality in contrast to the objectivism of modernistic thought. In the existential view, there is no objective reality grounded in natural laws that can be *discovered* through empirical processes. Instead, individuals *create* their own reality. Because of the relativity of reality, existentialists emphasized individual knowledge and personal choice. The subjectivism of the existentialists provided an alternative to the objectivism of the positivists.

Critical theory is another postpositivist philosophy that is a foundation for standards of complexity. Critical theory grew out of the Frankfurt School of Critical Theory that, from 1930 to the 1960s, critiqued the possibility of social change resulting from scientific research. The work of the Frankfurt School provided the foundation for the application of critical theory to education. This resulted in the reconceptualization or the broadening of what constitutes education and how education occurs (Pinar, Reynolds, Slattery, & Taubman, 1995). Some aspects of the reconceptualized view of education are that:

- Education is political in that dominant cultures attempt to reproduce their values by controlling the educational system.
- A study of education must include all of the influences on classrooms and schools, including popular culture, corporate culture, and any other aspects of the hidden curriculum that pervades the schools.
- The consequences of the educational process and the organization of educational structures must be interrogated in relation to concerns about social justice, an ethic of caring, and democratic participation.

Critical theorists who utilize a diversity of postpositivist analytical techniques to problematize modernistic educational structures promote a critical pedagogy rather than the technical pedagogy that is represented by a modernistic conception of education. Critical pedagogy expands the study of curriculum, instruction, and assessment to include the consequences of knowledge production, teaching, and learning for each individual within society.

Another important foundation for standards of complexity is the philosophy of pragmatism. American pragmatic philosophy grew out of the work of Charles Peirce, William James, and John Dewey. Essentially, pragmatism rejects the realistic idea that reality is based solely on natural laws and that knowledge is acquired solely through empirical research. Pragmatists see the nature of reality as ever changing due to the interaction of the individual with the environment. In other words, individuals *construct* knowledge and reality as they interact with their environment. This belief is in contrast to the realist belief that knowledge is absolute and can be discovered through empirical research or transmitted by an expert. Pragmatists believe that knowledge is individually and collectively constructed through this interaction. Dewey proposed that education should promote both critical thinking skills that would facilitate student's understanding of their interaction with the environment and scientific processes that would provide for a systematic examination of the environment.

In addition, Dewey promoted the idea that education should be used to improve the human condition. In the early twentieth century, Dewey and other proponents of this idea became known as progressives. Along with social reformers, and social meliorists, progressives criticized the positivistic views concerning the purpose and practice of education (Kliebard, 1995). They promoted the general view that society would be best served by an educational curriculum and system that was more child centered. Progressivism in education was an outgrowth of the larger progressive movement that was engaging in social and political reform during this time period and the pragmatist philosophy. Dewey (1916), as a pragmatist and progressive, promoted the idea that democracy and education were connected in that the purpose of education should be to promote American democracy. As a progressive and a pragmatist, Dewey focused on the consequences of educational practice. In this view, the desired consequences or outcomes of educational practice must inform and mediate the methods and practices of education. In Dewey's view, this critique of practice in relation to the consequences of practice must be grounded in how democracy is promoted by educational practice. Dewey's progressive background further grounded this critique of educational practice in values such as social justice and an ethic of caring.

Also, cognitive and developmental psychology is part of the foundation for standards of complexity. The ideas of individuals such as Jean Piaget and Lev Vygotsky about how a child's learning is mediated by cognitive and social development contribute to the pragmatist view of the social construction of knowledge. For instance, Vygotsky's contribution is significant because of his insight into the importance of the cultural setting in the development of thinking in children (Cole & Wertsch, 1996). According to Vygotsky, because of the social, cultural, and historical context of learning, genetically determined mental functions are not the sole mechanisms to be considered in our understanding of cognitive and moral development. Vygotsky's reasoning opened the door to an awareness of the culturally sensitive nature of an individual's construction of knowledge in that the cultural context of the learning environment can control the organization of knowledge, the communication of knowledge, and the authority and validation of knowledge (Cole, 1996; Daniels, 2001; Wertsch, 1985). Other social constructivists are grounded in Vygotsky's theory but place a greater emphasis on knowledge acquired through learning as a co-constructed activi-

ty by a community of participants (Lave, 1988; Lave & Wenger, 1991).

Proponents of **Critical constructivism** have critiqued traditional constructivist theory and view constructivism as embedded within a broad social, historical, and political context and believe that because of the sociocultural nature of learning, all learning is always political (Kincheloe, 1993). Critical constructivists maintain that to foster a connected and critical consciousness in students, teachers need to become critical researchers (Kincheloe, 1991) and transformative intellectuals (Giroux, 1993) who can critically engage their own socially constructed consciousness and utilize a critical pedagogy in their classrooms. Proponents of this view further argue that because of the connection of learning to the larger culture, a critical pedagogy must include the employment of cultural studies in order to better understand the role played by the larger culture in the learning that takes place in the classroom.

Research such as this has broadened the understanding of teaching and learning by including contexts or variables that are often considered irrelevant by modernistic thinking. To understand this broader context of education, postformal, or post modern inquiry is not restricted to quantifiable scientific methods but includes an eclectic array of information gathering and analytical techniques (i.e., qualitative methodologies, textual analysis, phenomenological analysis, critical hermeneutical analysis, semiotic analysis) that facilitate the acquisition of information about teaching and learning from a diversity of contexts, including social, cultural, economic, political, personal, and emotional (Kincheloe, 1998a).

All of this foundational thinking situates education as an inherently more complex activity than is proposed by modernistic thinking. In standards of complexity, curriculum, instruction, and assessment are not viewed as separate quantifiable activities but rather as dynamically interrelated activity that requires a broad understanding of how knowledge is produced, taught, and learned. In standards of complexity systems, curriculum is holistically viewed as interdisciplinary, not broken into discrete parts. Knowledge always changing and is produced when the individual interacts with the physical and cultural environment. The role of the teacher is to facilitate critical thinking in the students and to

Critical constructivism

a belief that knowledge does not exist in isolation from students but that students participate in the construction of knowledge, and that, when constructing knowledge, students need to be aware of the consequences of that knowledge in relation to issues of social justice, an ethic of caring, and democratic participation.

Complexity of student learning

an understanding that curriculum, instruction, assessment, and student learning are affected by psychological, cultural, social, economic, and political contexts.

help them acquire multiple methods of inquiry that facilitate their critical construction of knowledge. A critical problem solving permeates all instruction so that students are not only prepared for the inevitable change that they will experience but will also be critically aware of the consequences of their beliefs and actions. Assessment is multiple in order to capture the **complexity of student learning** and is authentic in that it attempts to assess student learning within real-life situations. Students are not ranked and sorted because of the unique context in which each student exists.

Two Distinct Views of the Nature and Purpose of Education

Technical standards and standards of complexity are based upon two very different philosophical foundations and view the nature and purpose of education in distinctively different ways. This difference can be seen in the debate that occurred in the beginning of the twentieth century between John Dewey and Edward Thorndike. The outcome of this debate was significant for education because it set the tone for how research, scholarship, theory, and practice would be defined and valued in education. As the scientific management philosophy became entrenched in education, the growing field of psychology also gained influence. At this time in order to be taken seriously as a science, the field of psychology strived to emulate the principles and practices of the established scientific fields. This attempt to be validated as a science resulted in the dominance of behavioral psychology. Thorndike, an influential behavioral psychologist, advocated an experimental and statistical basis for educational research. According to Thorndike, educational research was to follow the established scientific procedures of psychology, and only knowledge gained through quantifiable and statistically verified procedures conducted by certified experts would be considered appropriate as a basis for educational decision-making.

Coming from a pragmatic and critical foundation, Dewey proposed that education should be about helping children develop the skills and knowledge necessary to be effective democratic citizens. To accomplish this goal, children's learning should take place in educational environments that would be creative commu-

nities in that opportunities would be provided for children to learn necessary skills and knowledge but also to learn how to freely participate in a democratic society. To Dewey, education is more than learning the "material" it is also about promoting the development of an effective and efficient democratic society through the concomitant development of a free and critical citizenry. To achieve this goal, Dewey proposed that schools should mirror the kind of society that they wanted to achieve.

The difference between the positions held by Dewey and Thorndike had profound implications for the relationship between theory and practice, scholars and practitioners, the nature of educational research, curriculum, instruction, assessment, and the roles of all of the educational stakeholders. Ellen Lagemann (2000) provides a detailed discussion of this debate and the consequences of Thorndike's "win" and Dewey's "loss." Lagemann (2000) states that the "win" by Thorndike was the pivotal factor in the move by education away from close interactions between policy, theory, and practice and toward excessive quantification, scientism, and the resultant separation of theory and practice (p. xi).

This reductionism of educational theory and practice can be seen in Thorndike's belief that all human experience could be quantified through statistical analysis. His view of educational research required a controlled environment and the development of professional experts in scientific research methods and statistical analysis. These requirements meant that research needed to be contained in the laboratory, that a strict adherence to scientific and scholarly procedures was essential, and that professionals needed to be developed who were specialists in these procedures. The separation of theory and practice fostered by Thorndike's view reinforced the concurrent movement to scientifically manage the schools and the differentiation of educational roles. Professionalism came to mean that university professors would be trained to specialize in the generation of theory; school administrators would be trained to provide school leadership, and teachers would be trained to implement the theory and follow the dictates of the administrators. Distinctive professional boundaries, defined by advanced degrees and certifications, would be established to maintain the hierarchical structure.

Dewey's position put him in opposition to the structure of education at that time, while Thorndike's position was aligned with the promotion of the scientific management of schools. The significant difference between these two views of education can be seen in the theory, practice, and organization of Dewey's experimental school at the University of Chicago. In this school, the artificial dichotomies of theory and practice, scholars and practitioners, and male theorists and female practitioners were collapsed into an egalitarian community in which all professionals were scholars and practitioners or thinkers and doers. Instead of promoting a hierarchical separation of teachers and researchers, a separation of the disciplines, and a separation of professional roles, Dewey envisioned teachers-as-researchers, an interdisciplinary curriculum, and a sharing of the professional responsibilities for teaching and administrating. This view put Dewey clearly at odds with those who saw education as hierarchical, specialized, professionalized, and gendered, while Thorndike's position was aligned with the promotion of the scientific management of schools. Lagemann (2000) captures this distinction in her statement that "for Dewey, the study of education necessitated a partnership between and among many different people—a wide range of scholars and citizens as well as teachers, administrators, and parents; it could not be advanced through a hierarchy that differentiated among scholars, practitioners, and parents" (p. 50). Lagemann (2000) further summarizes the distinction between these two views in that "whereas Dewey's approach to educational study favored synthesis across disciplines and open communication and collaboration across roles and was therefore in opposition to advancing professionalization, Thorndike's approach advocated reliance on specialized expertise and fostered efforts to promote educational study as a professional science" (62).

The distinctive difference between these two views indicates that if Dewey had "won," today's educational system would be quite different. This difference also aligns with the inherently different purposes and nature of educational standards. Technical standards and accountability through standardized testing align with the view promoted by Thorndike, and standards of complexity are rooted in Dewey's pragmatic and progressive philosophy of education. These different approaches to standards and

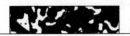

accountability can be seen in how each approach views curriculum, instruction, assessment, and the consequences of their approach.

Glossary

Best practice—curriculum, instruction, and assessment that can be supported by quantitative and qualitative research.

Centralized education—education that is controlled and standardized by a central authority such as the national government.

Complexity of student learning—an understanding that curriculum, instruction, assessment, and student learning are affected by psychological, cultural, social, economic, and political contexts.

Critical constructivism—a belief that knowledge does not exist in isolation from students but that students participate in the construction of knowledge, and that, when constructing knowledge, students need to be aware of the consequences of that knowledge in relation to issues of social justice, an ethic of caring, and democratic participation.

Decentralized education—all aspects of education are controlled by local communities.

Multiple assessment—the use of multiple techniques in the measurement of student achievement.

Scientific management of schools—the use and dominance of scientific and business principles in educational organization, management, teaching, and learning.

Standards-based education—when all aspects of an educational environment are focused on a set of guiding standards.

Teaching to the test—the singular use and prioritization of instructional strategies that are solely based on increasing student performance on a standardized test.

CHAPTER THREE

Technical Standards

Technical Standards and Curriculum

Disciplinary experts
individuals who have specialized knowledge in only one discipline, such as a specific form of mathematics, science, English, history, or any other field of knowledge. In contrast, educational generalists have a wide range of content and pedagogical knowledge that transcends disciplinary boundaries.

Value-neutral curriculum
the assumption that curriculum is an objective entity that is free of values. An opposing assumption is that curriculum is value laden, and the teaching of that curriculum includes the transmission of the attached values.

Concerning what constitutes valid knowledge, proponents of technical standards rely upon **disciplinary experts** to identify the essential knowledge of their fields. Scientists, mathematicians, historians, geographers, sociologists, psychologists, political scientists, language specialists, and other experts all are empowered to provide the specific content and skills that make up the mandated standards. These disciplinary experts pose their knowledge as scientifically based, empirically verified, measurable, and quantifiable. In addition, non-educators who represent special interest groups participate in this selection of valid and appropriate knowledge. In many cases, these content specialists are scholars who have little knowledge of the pedagogy that relates to K-12 students and how the identified knowledge interfaces with the unique contexts of their individual lives.

A technical standards-driven curriculum is posed as a **value-neutral curriculum.** However, others argue that the determination of appropriate content and skills is a political process that

reflects the values of the experts and the culture in which these experts are positioned. In a technical standards context, these disciplinary experts and the representatives of the special interests often represent the specific culture that currently dominates society. Therefore, the knowledge and skills that are selected as the content of the standards are a direct reflection of the values of the **dominant culture.** In this context, who produces knowledge, how knowledge is acquired, and the consequences of this knowledge are aligned with the values of the dominant culture. The focus on these unchallenged dominant representations erases other oppositional viewpoints, reproduces the status quo, and assumes that rights and privileges are naturally occurring and not assigned by one's position in society through gender, race, and social class (Berry, 2001, p. 307).

Because **disciplinary experts** make the curricular decisions, the curriculum of technical standards is reductionist. This means that facts and skills are viewed as individual phenomena that stand alone from the larger context in which they are nested. A reductionist curriculum is not interdisciplinary. History is essentially taught in isolation from other disciplines such as mathematics, science, and language arts. Fields that are somewhat related to history, such as geography, government, sociology, anthropology, and psychology, are ignored or peripherally included to support the learning of history. This fragmentation or splintering of the disciplines represents the fragmentation of how these disciplines are dynamically interrelated within real-life experiences (Jorgenson & Vanosdall, 2002). One outcome of this type of pedagogy is the reinforcement of a reductionist disciplinarity that denies students the opportunity to "work with big ideas, central organizing principles that have the power to generalize across experiences and disciplines" (Applefield, Huber, & Moallem, 2000/2001, p. 35). **Curricular fragmentation** of this kind is subject centered rather than child centered in that the subject is the center of the learning process rather that the child's understanding of the complexity of how the subject exists within a larger real-life context. Dewey (1963/1938) addressed this issue as the imposition of arbitrary adult authority upon the child. Dewey argued that both the experience of the adult and that of the child are essential elements in the learning process.

Dominant culture

The cultural knowledge and values of the group of individuals who politically and economically control society.

Disciplinary experts

Individuals who have specialized knowledge in only one discipline, such as a specific form of mathematics, science, English, history, or any other field of knowledge. In contrast, educational generalists have a wide range of content and pedagogical knowledge that transcends disciplinary boundaries.

Curricular fragmentation

When the complexity of curriculum is reduced to isolated disconnected parts.

Another curricular characteristic of technical standards is curriculum alignment. In **curriculum alignment**, the required content and skills are organized to promote efficient learning. With the intent of avoiding duplication, content and skills are assigned to each grade level. This assures that all standards will be taught and reinforced when necessary. Curriculum alignment is an outcome of the scientific management of schools and can be in the form of general organizational guidelines or a highly restrictive mandated sequence. Critics of this efficiency technique argue that when teachers are required to rigidly adhere to the scope and sequence of the curriculum, they are denied the flexibility to creatively facilitate student learning. In situations where teachers do not have the authority to deviate from the alignment plan, opportunities to build upon a "teachable moment" or to expand the context of what the student is learning are lost. Others argue that the act of aligning curriculum restricts student discovery and construction of knowledge. As mentioned, proponents of alignment argue that teacher autonomy in determining what is taught may interfere in the efficient presentation of all mandated curriculum and result in some test content not being covered.

Technical Standards and Instruction

The instruction within technical standards will be explored by looking at the instructional methods, instructional technology, the instructional schedule, the role of the teacher, professionalism and professional development, the role of the administration and the school board, and the role of the parents, community and students in relation to instruction.

Instructional Methods

Since performance standards are the focus of a technical standards system, instructional methods employed by the teachers must be tightly aligned with the performance standards. In this way, they function as a tight control mechanism over the teachers' ability to determine the curriculum and as an indirect control over the teachers' instructional practice. Teacher-centered and student-centered instruction can be used to teach the performance standards. However, assessment of the performance

standards, the other major component of the learning system, also greatly influences instructional methodology.

Schools that use a technical standards system have different degrees of instructional flexibility depending upon whether the summative assessment is a high-stakes exit-level standardized test, a grade-point average based on a compilation of teacher constructed tests, or multiple assessments that may include some type of testing, portfolios, and projects. If student achievement is measured by teacher tests or multiple assessments, teachers have a greater degree of flexibility in their instructional methods. If an exit-level test is used, then there is pressure to utilize instructional methods that have the greatest potential for achieving the mandated level of test scores. If test scores are disaggregated to reflect different demographic groups within the student population, the pressure to use repetitious remedial instructional methods for students at risk of failing the test increases.

In relation to the use of student-centered or teacher-centered instructional methods and their connection to the type of summative assessment, standardized testing tends to foster fewer student-centered methods than when other types of assessment are used. If teachers are determining whether students pass or fail, then teachers have more freedom in how they instruct the students and can employ more student-centered methods. If standardized tests are used to determine passing and failing, then the test content tends to at least influence or possibly drive the instruction. In this case, especially if the teachers are held personally responsible for the test results, a common response is to teach to the test and to use instructional methods that accommodate this practice. When test scores drop, the tendency is to default to direct instruction, rote learning, memorization, and test-taking skills. When teachers are in control of assessment, they can use the instructional methods that they determine will best accommodate student learning. In either case, the definition of what constitutes instructional "best practice" becomes relative to the type of assessment and the degree to which teachers are held accountable for student achievement.

Because of the NCLB mandate, schools will be assessing student achievement with standardized tests. Depending on how accountability for the test scores is handled, the instructional flexibility that teachers enjoy varies. In those schools that have instituted high-stakes exit level tests, instructional variables such as, student time on task, content coverage, and teaching to the test tend to become more important than others (Abrams & Madaus, 2003; Pedulla, 2003). Also in these classrooms, there tends to be a greater focus on students getting the right answer, the correct test answer, a more controlled use of higher-order- thinking skills, and an increase in lower-level thinking skills such as memorization, recall, and recognition. In addition, some instructional time devoted to learning the content and skill development is displaced by test question analysis activities, and activities designed to teach the students how to properly complete the test (such as how to correctly shade in the answer on the test). In some classrooms this instructional philosophy constitutes an endless cycle of predictable routines around categories laid out by companies dedicated to single-disciplinary study with subsequent assessment promoting a right/wrong binary (Sheehy, 2002). In addition, direct instruction models (Hunter, 1982; Rosenshine, 1988) that are highly directive in relation to teacher and student instructional activity guarantee time on task and content coverage. In a study of 2,500 teachers in Arizona, Haladyna, Nolen, and Haas (1991) found that reading, writing, and mathematics teachers lost at least 10 percent of their instructional time due to their focus on testing. These researchers identified a phenomenon that they called test pollution. They identified instructional practices that contaminated the external validity of the test—practices such as teaching test-taking skills, using practice tests, and engaging in student motivation activities prior to the test.

In a high-stakes testing environment such as Texas, students must be motivated to take the tests seriously. Throughout the school year and especially as the test draws near, Texas schools employ numerous motivational strategies. TAAS pep rallies, motivational speakers, school songs, games, and prizes are a few of the strategies that are used. Dallas Cowboy football players and cheerleaders lead the list of most-wanted speakers close to test time. A different motivational technique is to involve the parents in test preparation. Evening instructional sessions are offered to parents in which teachers provide training for the parents so that they can help prepare their children for the test. Many schools invite parents into the classrooms to serve as aids in test preparation activities. In addition to parental involvement, some schools urge

community organizations to coordinate their youth activities with the test dates and dates of important school test preparation activities (McNeil, 2000).

Many proponents of instruction within a technical standards learning system encourage the use of instructional best practice and do not promote teaching to the test. However, due to test pressure, many teachers feel compelled to use strategies that are the most efficient in relation to achieving high test scores. James Popham (2001) characterizes the most intense form of teaching to test as "drill and kill." In this technique, teachers engage their students in repetitious instructional activities that "transform their classrooms into cram-focused, assembly-line factories [that] risk extinguishing their students' love of learning" (Popham, 2001, p. 22). Popham further argues that teaching to the test encourages curriculum reductionism in that teachers teach what is tested and avoid what isn't. In this situation, non-tested content within their subject and other non-tested content areas, such as music, physical education, and art, decreases in importance or dropped from the curriculum.

Another aspect of the technical standards instructional system involves remediation. If students are not learning the required content or a certain amount of content in the prescribed time, remediation is needed (Gratz, 2000). Remediation can take place after the school day, outside of the assigned class time, or during the student's class. Some schools require all teachers, regardless of what subject they teach, to devote a portion of their instructional time to drill activities related to the test content. This practice tends to increase the closer the school comes to the test date. Regardless when the remediation occurs, the purpose of it is clearly to teach to the test. In Texas, a common remediation practice is to diagnostically categorize students as those who will pass the test, those "bubble students" who may pass the test with intensive remediation, and those who will assuredly fail the test. The "bubble students" are then assigned to teachers who provide special instruction during the regular class as well as in after-school programs.

In those schools that attempt to avoid teaching to the test, other instructional activities, such as cooperative learning, discovery, simulations, debates, concept attainment, projects, and research, tend to be tightly prescribed and controlled. This control is essential due to the need to cover content, to arrive at the "right" answer, and to stay within the time frame established by the testing schedule. Activities that encourage creativity, divergent thinking, and that expand the context of the curriculum are liabilities in a technical standards system that is driven by restrictive performance standards that are measured by standardized tests. If these activities are not controlled, they are seen as interruptions or shocks that are counter-productive to the technical standards learning process (Sheehy, 2002).

Instructional Technology

Instructional technology can range from audio-visual equipment and computers to chalkboards, textbooks, and teacher-constructed materials. Traditionally, instruction has been aided and influenced by textbooks. In the past, many teachers have relied upon textbooks and the instructional activities provided by the publisher. These supplemental resources include activities and questions included within the textbook, supplemental readings, worksheets, and assessments. Teachers often rely upon the text and these supplements to provide the organizational structure for their curriculum and instruction. With the movement toward mandated standards, some publishers have attempted to incorporate standards within their textbooks; however, it is difficult for a publisher to address all of the standards that are unique to each state. This lack of alignment between the text and the specific standards has required those teachers who use textbooks to also use additional commercially prepared supplementary materials that are focused on their state's specific test content or on test taking skills. In some cases, teachers develop their own supplemental materials that directly relate to their standards; however, this is time consuming for teachers, and costly for schools if they need to provide reimbursed professional development time for this purpose.

Standards-related materials also are in the form of computer programs, CD-ROMS, videos, and laser disks. These can perform either of two functions: act as a resource that only provides information or function as a teaching tool that provides direct instruction to the student. The former function requires the teacher to plan how the technology will be integrated into the instructional plan. The latter provides a predetermined learning

sequence that the student must follow and may limit teacher and student interaction. Most of the direct instruction software provides drill and practice for the student. Some schools use this direct instruction software as a means to control instruction in the classroom and as an efficient remediation tool. Direct instruction software in combination with scripted lesson plans (lesson plans that tell the teacher what to say and do within a designated time period) provides teacher-proof instruction and eliminates the teacher as a variable in the instructional process. This instructional strategy is in line with a factory system of education that utilizes mass production techniques in the learning process (Marshak, 2003). In an exit-test situation, this type of technology allows students to efficiently study the test content or to learn how to effectively take the test.

Other types of instructional software emulate the productivity software of the business community. The purpose of productivity software is not to teach the student but to increase the productivity of the student within the learning context (Tucker & Codding, 1998). Just as the word processor generates greater efficiency in the writing process, other productivity software functions in the same manner in other subjects. To enhance student productivity, this software efficiently eliminates repetitious activity that slows the learning process. To support a technical standards system, this software can be aligned with the performance standards and the standardized assessment. Many companies (Microsoft, Blackboard Inc., Plato Learning Inc., Intel, Pearson Technologies, Ezedia, Riverdeep Interactive Learning, Reliance Communications Inc.) are now entering this marketing niche by selling products that are directly related to the NCLB mandates (Walsh, 2003).

Proponents of this software warn that the "image of these technologies as a substitute for the teacher, delivering direct instruction to the student, is misleading and destructive" (Tucker & Codding, 1998, p. 99). They argue that a teacher is still needed to determine the "differences in how much a student knows, how the student has structured that knowledge, and the mental scaffolding available on which to build new knowledge" (Tucker & Codding, 1998, p. 99). However, to be appropriate for a technical standards instructional system that uses a standardized test, the software needs to reinforce the predetermined content, skills,

and values that are contained within the test, thus participating in the control of curriculum, instruction and student learning.

The Instructional Schedule

In a technical standards or results-oriented school, the organization of instructional time needs to efficiently reinforce the performance standards and guarantee that all aspects of the standards that may appear on a standardized test are covered. Once again, if a school's performance standards are not assessed through a standardized test, there is less pressure to implement a rigid school schedule. However, in all technical standards systems, there is a predetermined schedule that allows the efficient management of student learning. In Texas public schools, the testing dates influence the school schedule and pedagogical activities. All grades and subjects are affected by the impending test. In some schools, as test time nears, the school schedule is reorganized to provide structured time in all classes to prepare for the test. A significant amount of this instruction deals with drill and repetition, how to properly bubble in answers on the test, and the learning of mnemonic devices that will help a student narrow the possible answers and avoid distractor answers. Some schools designate time during the school day in which all teachers engage in test preparation activities. In addition, many schools require selected students to engage in tutorial activity after the formal school day. Another common practice is to give practice tests at least two or three times prior to the test. In this way, decisions can be made as how best to restructure the test preparation activities and to identify students who need intensive remediation.

The organization of a school schedule may vary within a technical standards environment, but there must be some organizational structure. These structures may include traditional 45-minute instructional blocks, larger blocks up to 90 minutes, or a flexible schedule that allows a redistribution of 10- or 15-minute blocks of instructional time to accommodate instructional methods that may vary within a short period of time. Since technical standards are based upon a concern for efficiency, instructional time most frequently occurs in some variation of the 45- or 90-minute instructional blocks.

The organization of instructional time affects instructional methods. The longer block allows more activities to take place

within the time period; however, proponents of this arrangement warn that teachers need to employ a diversity of instructional methods to offset student boredom (Canady & Rettig, 1996). Flexible schedules allow for the quick rearrangement of time to accommodate specific instructional activities; however, this requires a degree of instructional adaptability in the participating teachers and an empowerment of the teachers in structuring learning. Traditional shorter blocks restrict the use of instructional activities that require longer periods of time such as experiments, projects, and simulation gaming. Also, how instruction is scheduled impacts the learning environment. In traditional blocks of the 45-minute variety, instruction is more limited to the classroom, thus eliminating opportunities for instruction in places other than the classroom. In the end, the final consideration involving instructional schedules is how well the configured time facilitates the performance standards and the assessment method that measures student achievement.

The Role of the Teacher

An understanding of the teachers' role in a technical standards instructional system can be obtained with an analysis of their decision-making capacity, how professional expertise is defined, their position in the school hierarchy, how their professional effectiveness is evaluated, and the nature of their motivation.

In this kind of standards system, the capacity for teacher decision-making is restricted. Well-defined boundaries exist in relation to their capacity to make decisions concerning curriculum, instruction, and assessment. Teachers are not involved in the construction of the technical standards that drive the whole educational system. This level of decision-making is restricted to national or state experts. Within the classroom, teacher empowerment to deliver the curriculum also depends upon the type of accountability or assessment that is used. In non-high-stakes situations, teachers may have greater latitude in altering the curriculum and determining instructional strategies; however, they must still stay within the parameters set by the technical standards. In high-stakes situations, they are most often required to strictly adhere to the standards. As in curricular decision-making, teacher flexibility in determining classroom instruction and assessment also varies according to the type of final assessment. In some technical standards systems, teachers have a greater degree of decision-making concerning classroom instructional activities and assessments and in others must more closely adhere to instruction and classroom assessment that promote student achievement on the standardized test.

A definition of teacher professional expertise involves knowledge of content and pedagogy. Since content is organized by discipline, all technical standards systems require teachers to be content specialists instead of content generalists. Content specialists are experts in one subject and only teach in that subject area. Content generalists have professional knowledge in different subjects in order to teach content and skills in an interdisciplinary context. Pedagogically, all teachers are expected to display expertise in a diversity of instructional best practices unless they are teaching in a school that requires teacher-proof materials such as scripted lesson plans and programmed instruction materials. In situations like this teachers are pedagogical technicians who monitor the delivery of the prescribed curriculum. One result of schools that require narrow content and pedagogical specialization is the deskilling of teachers. **Deskilling** is a condition in which teachers do not need to learn or use a diversity of pedagogical skills or acquire a broad content-knowledge base. The deskilled teacher assumes a role similar to the semi-skilled blue-collar worker in a traditional assembly-line system of production. In this situation, there is no room for spontaneity in a teacher's response to student learning.

Deskilling

When teachers and other educational professionals become specialists with a narrow range of knowledge and skill. Deskilled teachers are low-level technicians who have little control over teaching and learning.

Once again in different types of technical standards systems, the professional expertise of the teachers is defined in different ways. However, this definition mirrors the nature of the technical standards. Since all technical standards are tightly focused on content, content knowledge and the efficient and effective delivery of content are the prime components in a definition of professional expertise. This focus on content is reinforced by states that provide alternative teacher certification programs that require an individual who wants to be a teacher to merely have an undergraduate degree and pass the appropriate standardized content test. In situations where a teacher may have to provide remediation out of the teacher's area of content specialization, teacher-proof instructional materials are used. In this situation, the

teacher becomes a technician who monitors student use of the materials.

Two final aspects of professional expertise in technical standards systems involve affect and ideology in the classroom. Students' emotional responses to the content are often viewed as an encumbrance in the learning process. Emotional responses by students consume instructional time and facilitate a broadening of the investigation into the topic under study. Once again, the more curriculum and instruction are focused on a high-stakes test, the more important it is to cover the prescribed material and to keep students on task. Also, a **critical interrogation** of the ideological and cultural interests that inform the interpretation of all subject matter is a problematic activity in a technical standards classroom. An examination by the student of how these interests affect the production of knowledge broadens student understanding and facilitates the development of critical participants in American democracy. However, this kind of critical interrogation becomes problematic when faced with time-on-task constraints and because the values reflected within the standards may be challenged.

The nature of a teacher's role in technical standards systems also becomes apparent when the position of the teacher in the educational hierarchy is explored. In technical standards systems, teachers have a well-defined position. External experts construct the standards, provide the instructional framework that best aligns with the standards, and provide the assessment instrument. Administrators function as managers who must make sure that teachers deliver the prescribed standards in an efficient manner. Administrators also evaluate the teachers based upon student achievement on the test. In some schools, selected teachers are part of leadership teams; however, even in this context their role is limited because all of the essential conditions have been predetermined.

The evaluation of teacher effectiveness is another indicator of the nature of a teacher's role. Technical standards systems define teacher effectiveness as accountability for student achievement on the exit test (Tucker & Codding, 1998). In states like Texas, the primary teacher evaluation criteria are set by the state and tied directly to student test achievement (Bertrand, 2001; Texas Education Agency, 2003). In fact, an individual teacher may

Critical interrogation

The use of inquiry methods that uncover the implications of a phenomenon related to social justice, an ethic of caring, and democratic participation.

exhibit a high degree of effectiveness but at the end of a school year receive a lower rating due to the school's low test performance. As in all standards systems, low-performing or unmotivated teachers are fired or encouraged to leave the profession. However, in technical standards driven schools, the low-performing category can include teachers who are instructionally very effective but resist some aspect of the standards system (Zehr, 2003).

In all standards systems, teacher motivation is important. Teachers can be intrinsically or extrinsically motivated. In technical-standards systems that restrict teacher autonomy, motivation becomes a problem when some teachers resist the system. In these situations, teachers need to be externally motivated. Some schools offer staff incentives that can be in the nature of financial rewards, release time, or additional instructional materials. Other schools simply motivate through the evaluation process. In either case, the focus is on extrinsic motivation. The need for extrinsic motivation is akin to the same need that occurs in industry to motivate disempowered, disenfranchised, and bored workers. Teachers are encouraged to be life-long learners and to engage in professional development; however, in a technical standards system, what you learn and how you learn it are also constrained by the standards that drive the school system.

In relation to the affective component of teacher motivation, a study of a northern school and a southern school detailed the negative emotions experienced by teachers in high-stakes testing situations (Smith, 1991; Smith & Rottenburg, 1991). These researchers reported that many teachers experienced feelings of shame, guilt, anger, and embarrassment over the impact of the testing program on their students and on their own teaching. Linda McNeil (2000) found that one significant effect of the Texas standardized testing program was the depersonalization of the teachers as they acted to meet the required student achievement levels on the test.

Professionalism and Professional Development

How teacher professionalism is defined helps us understand the role of the teacher within a technical standards instructional system. As previously described, in technical standards systems, teachers function within well-defined professional boundaries.

Hierarchically positioned, teachers have little power and, in some cases, assume the role of a deskilled technician. In this context, the teachers' level of professionalism is directly defined by their ability to deliver the prescribed standards and how well their students do on a standardized test. This definition of professionalism has implications for how teachers compare to other professionals and the public perception of the teacher as a professional. Some argue that the more teachers become deskilled technicians, the lower the public's perception of the profession becomes. This has further implications concerning teacher reimbursement and the attraction of bright, motivated, and creative individuals into the profession.

Another implication involves the retraining of current teachers. Professional development is a requirement for all teachers in all systems; however, in a technical standards system, the restrictive nature of professional development also impacts teachers' sense of their own professional level. In technical standards systems, professional development is focused solely on the standards and student mastery of the standards. Tucker and Codding (1998), who have been instrumental in the development and promotion of the New Standards, clearly represent the restrictive nature of professional development. In a discussion about improving school performance they state that "analyzing student work and student performance and benchmarking practices—are also among the most effective approaches to professional development for the instructional staff. The first requires teachers to examine their own practices very carefully in relation to the progress that their students are making against the standards; the second gets them into the mode of searching everywhere for the practices most likely to help them meet the student needs that the first activity reveals" (Tucker & Codding, 1998, p. 120).

Their position is well taken within the context of a technical standards system because what the teachers learn in their professional development aligns with the requirements of the system. However, others argue that in this case there is a lack of teacher self-directed learning toward what the individual teachers deem necessary to be more complete professionals. In this kind of system, teachers can still pursue what they individually deem as professionally relevant study, but if what they pursue does not align with the standards, then it may become irrelevant. In this case, the issue becomes who should decide what professional development is relevant, and to whom it must be relevant? In technical standards systems, the answer is that it must be relevant to the standards, not to the individual teacher's view of what is best for the teacher, the teacher's students, and the community in which the school resides.

Besides their own schools, regional support organizations, colleges, and universities provide teacher professional development. Regional organizations are generally funded by the state or the local school districts, and the training that they provide is usually closely aligned with mandated state standards. The independence of colleges and universities is decreasing as far as the educational philosophy, curriculum, and instructional strategies they provide in teacher professional development programs. Their autonomy is being continuously eroded because of the demands placed upon the public schools to which the universities must respond or become irrelevant to the needs of the public schools. Also, in some states, in order to maintain their ability to certify preservice teachers and to grant master's degrees, universities must conform to the technical standards that become part of the state mandates for universities.

As an example of the impact of technical standards on professional development, in Texas, teacher in-service and professional development is greatly affected by the technical standards and accountability system. Due to the importance of the test results, significant amounts of in-service time are devoted to the main function of the school—guaranteeing appropriate student achievement levels on the test. Topics related to the standards and their accountability tests dominate the in-service agendas.

The Role of the Administration and the School Board

School administrators play a diversity of roles that are social, business, cultural, political, and educational in nature. Administrators are accountable for all aspects of their educational system, not limited to but including the fiscal health of the school or district, management of the educational staff and support personnel, public relations, curriculum, instruction, assessment, educational best practice, school safety, the academic and vocational achievement of all types of students, extracurricular

activities, and the school or district culture. They are held account-able to school board regulations and procedures; by the degree of support provided by their students, teachers, and parents; to community groups and other special interests that include religious groups, business groups, athletic booster clubs, Parent Teacher Associations; to federal mandates that are legislated or attached as conditions of federal funding; to state requirements involving all aspects of the educational operation; for student achievement as measured by student success after graduation, student performance on standardized tests such as the SAT and ACT; by regional voluntary accrediting organizations; and, by the media representations of their personal effectiveness and student and school performance. In a technical standards system, additional accountability is imposed by the state and federal standards and assessments. In the context of this plethora of accountability structures, public school leaders face multiple, simultaneous obligations that often conflict (Shipps & Firestone, 2003), that create an impossible role for educational leaders (Archer, 2003b).

Administrators do not have the job security that is provided by tenure or unions and can be terminated at the discretion of the school board. Therefore, administrators need to be sensitive and highly responsive to their responsibilities and accountability structures. In technical standards systems driven by high-stakes tests, administrative accountability is essentialized into one indicator—the school or district's test results. All other accountability measures continue to measure their effectiveness; however, successful performance as determined by these indicators is overshadowed by the test results. In high-stakes testing states, such as Texas, administrative effectiveness is primarily defined as student test achievement, and administrators may be terminated based upon poor student test scores.

In addition, administrators function as instructional leaders. A main aspect of their job is to either set or facilitate the development of the educational philosophy that is the foundation of their school or district culture. Because of individual administrative philosophies or the uniqueness of the local community, the educational philosophies may vary from school to school. In technical standards systems, these individual or locally responsive philosophies tend to reflect, to some degree, the philosophy of the imposed system. For instance, in a high-stakes testing environment, local choice of educational philosophy must align with the philosophy of the technical standards, or the school risks suffering the negative consequences if their elected philosophy fails to meet the state and federal outcomes. Therefore, the effect of technical standards measured by exit tests tends to standardize the educational philosophies, the resultant educational cultures, and the administrative practice of schools.

In technical standards systems, local school boards also lose a degree of their autonomy. School boards still perform their legislated functions and have the latitude to set educational policy; however, especially when high-stakes testing is the mandated accountability measure, they feel the pressure to conform to the policies that best meet the mandated student achievement levels. For instance, in Texas, local responsibility is defined as implementing the state system of standards and accountability. The local school boards are left only with the power to carry out the state mandates. All power and major decision-making is centralized in the state. Of course, with the power of the state mandates, local decision making that is not directly related to curriculum and instruction is indirectly further controlled by the limited options allowed by the intense need to meet the state mandates. For example, a local school could decide to also implement a portfolio system; however, the test is what counts, and if the portfolio system does not directly relate to appropriate student achievement on the test, the portfolio system is essentially rendered irrelevant to the needs of the school.

Also in states such as Texas, there are even standards for individual school board members that require a specified amount of inservice training related to the state standards. Being elected officials, they do not lose their position if they do not comply, but their inservice record does become part of the public record (Lowery & Buck, 2002). Technical standards systems are called systems because all educational stakeholders and all aspects of a school's environment are controlled by philosophy represented by the standards.

The Role of the Parents, the Community, and the Students

In technical standards systems, the parents' role is to reinforce the school's curriculum and instruction that is designed to ensure

appropriate student test scores. Parents are strongly encouraged to monitor their children's out-of-school study. One instructional technique that is highly promoted is an increase in student homework. Of course, the effectiveness of homework depends upon the available time and the ability of the parents to supervise this task. In the families situated within the higher socioeconomic levels, the nature of the family and the educational level of the parents can accommodate this extension of schoolwork into family time. However, because of lower levels of parental education, parents and students in lower socioeconomic levels struggle to meet the time demands of homework. One attempt to overcome this difficulty is to structure homework as repetitive activities involving lower-level thinking skills, such as memorization and comprehension. Some conservative proponents of technical standards, such as the Brookings Institution, argue that there is not enough homework and that more needs to be given to bolster the current standards and accountability reform (Brookings Institution, 2003). Liberal proponents of technical standards maintain that because of the diverse family socioeconomic contexts, longer school days and school years are the proper reinforcements for this reform (Buell & Kralovec, 2003).

The community also plays intentional and unintentional roles in supporting technical standards. Community groups are encouraged to provide instructional materials, tutoring, and incentives for student achievement of the standards. The economic focus of technical standards encourages business groups to deliver formal instruction, such as the Junior Achievement programs, in the public schools. When standardized tests are the main accountability mechanism, community groups are encouraged to arrange the schedules of their youth activities to accommodate the testing dates. In some school districts, community groups are solicited to provide rewards, prizes, and motivational speakers prior to the test. One motivational technique is to involve the parents and community members in test preparation. Evening instructional sessions are offered to adults in which teachers provide training for them so that they can help prepare students for the test. Many schools invite adults into the classrooms to serve as aids in test-preparation activities.

Communities have a vested interest in promoting the standards and successful student test achievement. In states that have

accountability measures that include the dissolution of the local school board, the dissolution of the school district as an independent district, or the privatization of the schools, the identity of the local community is at stake. In states that require publication of school test scores, real estate values of areas of the school district may be affected by the low-performance of a neighborhood school.

Finally, students are most affected by technical standards and their rigid enforcement through high-stakes tests. Students who perform poorly on a test may not be allowed to pass to the next grade level or to receive a high school diploma. In either case, this practice has significant effects on the student's personal identity, self-esteem, and future position in society (Neill, 2003). Some states with high-stakes tests experience high attrition rates of students in certain demographic levels (Amrein & Berliner, 2002; Freeland & Tucci, 2003). For instance in Texas, despite low state reported **dropout rates,** certain groups of students continuously experience high attrition rates (Cárdenas, 1998; Johnson, 1999; Suval, 1999; Viadero, 2000). An accounting technique used by the Texas Education Agency, called leaver coding, masks the true attrition rate of Hispanic, African American, and white low socioeconomic students. Leaver codes (Archer, 2003a; Texas Education Agency, 2003) describe the circumstances in which students leave the public school system. Many of the coded reasons allow schools not to officially count students who left as school dropouts. Analyses of student attrition in relation to leaver coding find that actual attrition rates for these student groups range from 35 percent to 50 percent (Johnson, 1999).

In addition to at-risk students, other students may experience negative consequences. For instance, in 2003, 43,000 children in Florida and 11,700 Texas students repeated third grade after failing to meet state mandates; in addition, 18,000 of Louisiana's fourth and eighth graders were also held back (Reid, 2003). Research shows that many students who are retained in a grade level eventually become school dropouts (Fisher, 2000; Klein, Hamilton, McCaffrey, & Stecher, 2000; Yardley, 2000). Other negative consequences occur in schools that focus exclusively on the tested information. In this case, curriculum can be "dumbed down" or displaced (Charlesworth, Fleege, and Weitman, 1994; Haladyna, Nolen, and Haas, 1991)). A dumbing down of the

Dropout rates

The number or percentage of students who do not complete an educational program. Dropout rates can be defined in many ways. Student dropouts may be coded differently and not included in the dropout rate. A more accurate assessment of student failure to finish an educational program is student attrition. Student attrition simply compares the number of students who started school in kindergarten with the number who did not graduate from any school.

curriculum occurs when all students experience an increase in repetitious test-oriented instruction at the expense of a loss of other curriculum and an emphasis on test-oriented instruction. In schools such as this, non-tested curriculum, within a subject or subjects that are not tested, is replaced by additional instruction on the tested information. For instance, in Texas, a plethora of commercial materials is available (e.g., Book and Brain for TAAS, Breaking the TAAS Code, TAAS Coach). They replace course materials that are related to the teaching and understanding of the disciplinary content. The students who are most insulated from dumbing down and curriculum displacement are those in the advanced courses. Another negative consequence is that more students leave formal schooling in order to earn a General Educational Development (GED) credential (Murnane, Willett, & Tyler, 2000). In this case, the GED certification facilitates entry into lower-level occupations but restricts the students' acquisition of the knowledge, skills, and attitudes that can enrich their lives.

Technical Standards and Assessment

Generally, the assessment of technical standards involves the use of standardized testing, with many states moving to their use as high-stakes exit-level tests. Proponents of high-stakes tests find them appealing because they can be used to monitor state and local compliance with national mandates, greatly influence state policy when scores are low as a result of reduced federal funding, influence the behavior of all educational stakeholders, influence the way the public perceives public schools, appear to be scientific, and therefore, valid measurements of student achievement, and facilitate the cost-benefit analysis of public education (Natriello & Pallas, 2001).

The Importance of Cutscores, Percentiles, and Stanines

Opponents of high-stakes testing tend to focus on the arbitrary nature of the setting of the tests' **cutscores** or passing scores. Most of the high-stakes tests used by states are criterion-referenced tests in that student scores are related to student performance of the standards. The performance standards explicitly describe what students need to do. On the corresponding test, a cutscore, or a number on a score scale that determines whether the student passed or failed the standard, determines student

Cutscores
a number on a score scale that determines whether the student has passed of failed a standard.

mastery of the standards. Since there are degrees of student performance of a standard, the cutscore is an estimation of what constitutes acceptable and unacceptable performance. A cutscore of 70 that indicates passing or failing is an arbitrary decision that does not consider the small performance difference between scores of 67 to 73. Cutscores can represent minimum competencies, high competencies, or can be increased with each administration of the test. Common cutscore designations include below basic, basic, proficient, or advanced competency.

Therefore, opponents argue that the severe consequences that students can suffer by failing a high-stakes test or achieving a lower level of competency are connected to the intent and values of the individuals who set the cutscore. Cutscores represent the judgments of those individuals who determine whether student performance was indeed adequate and are essentially more important than the performance standard. One testing scholar states "these decisions could be changed, and often are changed, when made by different persons, at different times, or under different circumstances. The cutscore could always be moved up or down a bit without violating any fundamental principles. We create the standard, there is no gold standard for us to find, and the choices we make about where to set the standard are matters of judgment" (Kane, 2001, p. 83).

Stanines

a one to nine scale of percentages that are used to rank student performance on a standardized test to the performance of other students.

In norm-referenced tests, percentiles and **stanines** are used to rank students. If a student scores in the 70th percentile, then that means that 30% of the students scored higher. Stanines are a scale of 1 to 9 with each number representing a different percentage (i.e., 1 = 4%, 2 = 7%, 3 = 12%, 4 = 17%, 5= 20%, 6 = 17%, 7 = 12%, 8 = 7%, and 9 = 4%). In any case, the quality of the student performance is determined by its relationship to the performance of other students. Percentiles and stanines do not provide information about the student's performance of the standard's criteria. A student could meet the requirements of the standard but rank low if other students exceeded the standard's criteria.

Shortcomings in Measuring Student Performance

James Popham (2001) identifies two shortcomings in the use of standardized tests to measure the quality of student performance and teacher instruction. First, Popham identifies

teaching/testing mismatches (pp. 43–46). In this mismatch, what is covered on the test may not be emphasized in the local curriculum. Since textbooks are the most frequently used resource, they greatly influence the content covered in the class. Popham (2001) reports that in a comparison of the leading elementary mathematics textbooks with the content of one of the nation's leading standardized tests, "investigators discovered that in the case of *every* standardized test, at least 50 percent of the content was not addressed meaningfully in any textbook. For some of the tests examined, fully 80 percent of the content was not addressed meaningfully in *any* textbook" (p. 44). Proponents of standardized testing would argue that this can be corrected by either teaching to test, using commercial materials that relate directly to the test, using teacher-constructed materials based on the test, or teaching test-taking skills that increase the probability of a correct guess.

Another shortcoming identified by Popham deals with test reliability or the degree to which the test can be consistently generalized to different schools within a state or the nation. If a test is valid only for certain suburban schools, then its use in rural and urban schools is problematic. To enhance reliability, test makers strive to create a wide score-spread. The more spread out the scores, the more test scores can be used to contrast test takers. Score-spread is enhanced by eliminating answers that are too easy. "There's a tendency to remove from standardized achievement tests any item on which students perform too well" (Popham, 2001, p. 55). Popham (2001) states that because of score-spread "as a perverse consequence, items covering the most important things that teachers teach tend to be excluded from standardized achievement tests" (p. 48). In other words, students who effectively learned significant parts of the standards may still score low on the test because what they learned isn't tested. Some states that use high-stakes tests periodically revise the test content or raise the cutscores when too many students score high on the test. For instance, Texas has continuously revised their state test from the TABS, to the TEAMS, to the TAAS, to the TAKS (Horn, 2003). Proponents of this practice maintain that they are consistently raising the standards; however, this practice challenges the validity of the tests as year-to-year comparisons of student achievement.

Another reliability and validity concern about standardized tests is that not all high-stakes exit-level tests being used by the states are statistically supported as reliable and valid. In these cases, significant decisions about student achievement, educator effectiveness, and school effectiveness are based upon unsupported tests. Klein, Hamilton, McCaffrey, and Stecher (2000) compared the Texas TAAS results with NAEP test results and found that over a four-year period the interpretation of the success of fourth grade testing by Texas state officials differed from what the NAEP reported. In this study the gap in achievement among racial and ethnic groups was reported by Texas to be smaller and decreasing; however, the NAEP results indicated that the gap was actually large and increasing slightly. This kind of disparity in the analysis of the test results raises further questions about the effectiveness and efficiency of the use of a standardized test as the sole determinant of student learning and teacher effectiveness. Later studies (Haney, 2000; Hoffman, Assaf, & Paris, 2001) raised further questions about the validity of the test and the accuracy of the analysis of the test results.

Equity and Ethics

Any discussion of equity and ethics in education starts with the purpose of education. As previously discussed, the purposes that drive technical standards and standards of complexity systems are inherently different in the kind of society that is to be constructed. However, despite these differences in purpose, how these purposes are reached and the consequences of the implementation of these methods on all individuals must be scrutinized in relation to concerns about equity and ethics. The implementation of technical standards has become tightly linked to the use of high-stakes standardized tests. The use of these tests and their effects on various individuals have raised significant concerns about the equitable nature of these tests.

The issue of equity in relation to high-stakes standardized tests is a consideration of how different groups of individuals are advantaged and disadvantaged by these tests. Numerous studies have raised the concern that this type of accountability is inequitable for certain social class, racial, and ethnic groups. In relation to social class, numerous studies have shown a direct correlation between socioeconomic status and test scores (Berliner &

Biddle, 1996; Jencks, 1972; Sacks, 1999). In other words, the lower one's socioeconomic status, the greater the chance of attaining a low score. Intertwined with socioeconomic status is the race and ethnicity of the test taker. Once again, government statistics and scholarly studies show a direct correlation between these demographic groups and poor school and test performance (Jencks & Phillips, 1998; Longstreet, 1973; Madaus & Clarke, 2001; McNeil, 2000; Orfield & Wald, 2000; Sacks, 1999; Sauer, 2003; Spring, 1989, 2001; Valenzuela, 1999, 2000).

Various explanations are offered for this correlation between low test scores and these groups. One explanation is that these groups tend to receive fewer educational opportunities and a less rigorous education due to "less-experienced teachers, a more remedial-type curriculum, larger classes and less individualized attention, lower expectations for students of color, and overall fewer resources in the school" (Swope & Miner, 2000a, p. 11). Another deals with the issue of cultural bias in the construction of test questions. Many scholars have shown that the validity of the test is skewed when test content is framed within examples and terminology taken from middle and upper social classes. In this case, students from lower socioeconomic levels have no frame of reference for the context in which the content is posed and therefore select the wrong answer, not because they can't perform the task, but because they do not understand the question's cultural context. In addition, language bias occurs on tests that require English-as-second-language students to take a test that is linguistically European and Anglo-Saxon based. In this case, the test is primarily measuring their ability to understand this type of language rather than their ability to respond to the content and skills. Also, psychological research has shown that different groups of individuals have different cognitive styles (Woolfolk, 2004). In this case, since most tests reflect a linear mode of thinking and students who represent other learning styles are handicapped in their test performance.

Related to these concerns about equity is the issue of educational ethics. It is well documented that students from lower social classes, non-white demographic groups, and non-European-based cultures have higher dropout rates and greater grade-level retention rates than other students. Many scholars argue that high-stakes test pressure exacerbates this educational outcome. In states like Texas that have instituted this kind of testing, student dropout rates for these groups have risen (Cárdenas, 1998; Horn, 2001b; Johnson, 1999; Madaus & Clarke, 2001; Suval, 1999; Viadero, 2000; Valenzuela, 1999, 2000). This raises the ethical concern about the appropriateness of an educational policy that has such a significant deleterious effect on a large student population. In fact, the issue of test validity and the discriminatory effect of the test on certain demographic groups became an issue in a lawsuit filed against the state of Texas by several students who were denied a diploma because of their test scores. The court conceded that the Texas test, the TAAS, had discriminatory consequences for African American and Hispanic students but ruled in favor of the state (GI Forum, 1999, 2000; Horn, 2001c). The court's position was that the state had the constitutional right to establish educational policy as long as the policy did not egregiously violate federal law.

Many scholars have argued that educational phenomenon such as dropping out of school or being retained in a grade level are directly related to the cultural capital (Bourdieu & Passeron, 1977) that students bring to school from their family. The idea of cultural capital is that all aspects of human behavior within a society are judged in relation to their value in helping the individual become part of the mainstream and subsequently reaping the rewards of that position in society. Cultural capital ranges from study habits, prior knowledge and skills, to the ability to act, speak and dress "appropriately." Low socioeconomic groups and groups that are marginalized from mainstream culture tend to have less appropriate cultural capital than other individuals who are culturally and socially better positioned. Those who culturally dominate society define what constitutes educational appropriateness. In America, this definition tends to be constructed in the context of Western European, white, male, and middle-class beliefs, values, and opinions. Students who deviate from this cultural construct have additional hurdles to overcome. As children from the dominant and subordinate cultures begin school, the former start with numerous advantages while the latter start with a cultural deficit. Programs like Head Start and other prekindergarten and K-3 programs attempt to help students overcome this cultural deficit. However, many individuals argue that proponents of technical-standards-driven standardized testing

focus on the individual efficacy of students instead of recognizing this cultural deficit. The outcome of this belief in relation to equality and ethics is that in technical standards systems with high-stakes accountability testing many of these marginalized students begin school with a high potential for failure rather than for success.

Another area of ethical concern deals with instructional practice that is focused on test preparation. Haladyna, Nolen, and Haas (1991) discuss the degree of ethicality in relation to certain instructional practices. They argue that the following practices are educationally unethical: developing a curriculum based on the content of a test, preparing objectives based on items on the test and teaching accordingly, presenting items similar to those on the test, using commercially prepared test preparation materials or other score-boosting activities, dismissing low-achieving students on testing day to artificially boost test scores, and presenting items verbatim from the test to be given. In relation to instructional ethics, Peter Sacks (1999) provides a detailed discussion of how in 1988 North Carolina constructed a testing code of ethics that agreed with the assessment ethics provided by Haladyna, Nolen, and Haas, and, later in 1996, after student test achievement became problematic, revised the code without any mention of the ill-effects of teaching to the test (pp. 123–124). Many proponents of technical standards recognize the unethical practice of teaching to the test and maintain that best practice instruction will guarantee appropriate levels of student test achievement. However, the high-stakes nature of standardized testing creates an inordinate pressure on educators to engage these less ethical instructional practices.

In addition to the ethics of teaching to the test, test performance pressure has resulted in overt acts of cheating. In high-stakes testing states, numerous acts of cheating on tests have been reported (Hartocollis, 1999, 2000; Hoff, 2003; Low & Horn, 2001; Trotter, 2003). Cheating occurs in numerous forms, such as answers being given to the students, answers being erased and replaced with correct answers, administrative tampering with test scores, providing extra time for timed tests, changing student identification numbers on tests, coaching students during the test, reading the test questions to some students, and, in cases where special education is exempt from the test, labeling students as such to prevent them from taking the test. Besides these egregious examples of cheating, other actions are ethically suspect, such as firing teachers who refuse to teach to the test or retaining students who are at-risk of passing the test to increase their preparation for the test. Many educators believe that their only viable response to the pressure of the mandates is "to game the system by engaging in practices that pump up numerical outcomes but undermine the academic interests of students—narrowly teaching to the test, completely ignoring nontested subjects, fudging the numbers, or even encouraging certain students to stay home on test day or drop out altogether" (Jerald, 2003, pp. 13–14). Of course, this response is ethically fraught with peril.

Whether consideration of the effects of high-stakes testing on certain demographic groups, the promotion of one view of what constitutes American culture over others, teaching to the test, or cheating on the test, concerns about equity and ethics in relation to high-stakes testing of technical standards need to be considered in relation to any educational purpose. Certainly, the practice of punishing low-performing schools and rewarding high-performing schools is ethically suspect in relation to the previously discussed factors.

Student Motivation and Emotional Response

Many individuals suggest that the stated goal of all educators regardless of their position on standards and accountability is to facilitate the development of students as life-long learners. To achieve this goal requires motivating students to develop a life-long love of learning. Obviously, a significant factor in student motivation is students' emotional response to school and learning. Numerous studies and our own personal experience with standardized testing suggest that the outcome of this type of assessment is usually, at best, heightened anxiety and, at worst, feelings that range from shame and guilt to low levels of self-worth and self-esteem. Many individuals can attest to the test anxiety that surrounded college entrance standardized tests and the impact of their test performance on their personal identity.

This kind of emotional response and motivational impact also occurs in many students who are in a K-12 high-stakes testing environment. Susan Wilde (2002 argues that "tests, particularly when heavily emphasized, lead students to feel anxious,

inadequate, or disillusioned more than a regular day in school does" (p. 13). Alfie Kohn (1993) extensively discusses this issue of motivation in traditional technical standards systems. Regarding the use of standardized tests, students experience a plethora of negative feelings when they are labeled as deficient or bad students because of their performance on a standardized test. Studies involving the Massachusetts Comprehensive Assessment System indicate that a large percentage of students expressed feelings of anxiety, anger, boredom, and pessimism about the test; and tended to withdraw from the testing situation (Wheelock, 2003; Wheelock, Bebell & Haney, 2000). These studies also identified patterns of student behavior that challenge the belief that the high-stakes nature of the test enhances student motivation and effort in a uniform way. Peter Sacks (1999) reports, "test-driven classrooms exacerbate boredom, fear, and lethargy, promoting all manner of mechanical behaviors on the part of teachers, students, and schools, and bleed schoolchildren of their natural love of learning" (pp. 256–257). Since standardized tests are the only important accountability measure in many schools, the effects of other assessments that indicate positive student performance are negated. Successful performance in class activities, teacher praise, and letter grades provide little positive emotional support for students in light of the results of the official test. In one Texas elementary school, the principal initiated the practice of posting each class's scores on the standardized test. Besides the questionable legality of this practice, individual teachers and students who did not do well on the test may experience negative personal feelings and negative reactions from other teachers and students in the school (Galley, 2003; Jones, Jones, Hardin, & Chapman, 1999).

An additional emotional effect on students relates to the fact that test results are disaggregated by demographic categories. Pressure is placed on the school to ensure passing rates for all students; however, a low ranking of the school due to poor performance by one or two demographic groups focuses all of the resultant emotions on those individuals in the low-performing groups. In the context of higher education, this creates the potential for exclusionary entrance requirements as well as remediation for African Americans, Hispanics, and individuals who are economically disadvantaged and who consistently score low as a subgroup. In public schools, regardless of how individual states decide to report student test scores, the Leave No Child Behind Act (United States Department of Education, 2002) requires all districts to provide to the public an annual report of student achievement scores disaggregated by race, gender, English Language Proficiency, disability, and socio-economic status by the 2005–2006 school year. When the federal and state governments require disaggregated test results, they are focusing the responsibility for learning solely on the individual student and the student's school. This conservative focus diverts the public's attention from the multitude of larger societal situations and conditions (e.g., educational funding, poverty, drug abuse, school safety, racism, classism, sexism) that are not under the control of the individual or the school but are significant variables that affect student performance on a test. In addition, they focus the negative consequences for the school and the school's community on those individuals who failed the test, thus creating the potential for significant negative emotional responses in those individual students and in the community toward those students.

There is a growing concern that proponents of standardized test-based technical standards systems "have not paid enough attention to who will be motivated and who will not" (Madaus & Clarke, 2001, p. 97). This becomes an important consideration when students make conclusions concerning the connection between passing the test and the future benefits that may occur because of the passing of the test. Some students "while believing they may have the ability to pass, are not motivated to work toward examination success because they do not see the test credential necessarily resulting in jobs or college because of scarcity, competition, or lack of relevance in their social setting" (Madaus & Clarke, 2001, p. 97). In addition, "drill and kill" instructional strategies further disconnect students from seeing learning as a personally worthwhile activity.

Technical standards systems that are test driven tend to rely on extrinsic motivational techniques that do little to develop the intrinsic motivation that is necessary for the development of lifelong learning. If student test achievement is focused on material rewards, such as prizes or time off from school, students associate school and learning with the rampant materialism that is a large part of American society. Learning for material gain may dis-

place learning for learning's sake. Whether a student becomes extrinsically motivated or loses motivation and drops out of school, the negative motivational aspects of a standardized testing climate only succeed in alienating students from the goal of becoming life-long learners.

Glossary

Critical interrogation—the use of inquiry methods that uncover the implications of a phenomenon related to social justice, an ethic of caring, and democratic participation.

Curricular fragmentation—when the complexity of curriculum is reduced to isolated disconnected parts.

Curriculum alignment—when the written curriculum is the taught curriculum and the tested curriculum.

Cutscores—a number on a score scale that determines wheterh the student has passed of failed a standard.

Deskilling—when teachers and other educational professionals become specialists with a narrow range of knowledge and skill. Deskilled teachers are low-level technicians who have little control over teaching and learning.

Disciplinary experts—individuals who have specialized knowledge in only one discipline, such as a specific form of mathematics, science, English, history, or any other field of knowledge. In contrast, educational generalists have a wide range of content and pedagogical knowledge that transcends disciplinary boundaries.

Dominant culture—the cultural knowledge and values of the group of individuals who politically and economically control society.

Dropout rates—the number or percentage of students who do not complete an educational program. Dropout rates can be defined in many ways. Student dropouts may be coded differently and not included in the dropout rate. A more accurate assessment of student failure to finish an educational program is student attrition. Student attrition simply compares the number of students who started school in kindergarten with the number who did not graduate from any school.

Stanines—a one to nine scale of percentages that are used to rank student performance on a standardized test to the performance of other students.

Value-neutral curriculum—the assumption that curriculum is an objective entity that is free of values. An opposing assumption is that curriculum is value laden, and the teaching of that curriculum includes the transmission of the attached values.

Standards of Complexity

Standards of Complexity and Curriculum

Curriculums containing standards of complexity are viewed as curriculums of complexity in that they attempt to facilitate student understanding of the complex context in which knowledge and skills are nested. Knowledge is not viewed as fragments within isolated disciplines but as socially constructed information that is connected to the students' own experience. In this context, curriculum is viewed as a dynamic ever-changing process as students critically interrogate the information and the assumptions upon which the information is based. The purpose of curriculum based upon standards of complexity is to facilitate student identification and critical interrogation of the complex context of phenomena through the employment of higher-order thinking skills. Instead of memorizing facts and demonstrating skills in a restricted context, standards of complexity focus on holistic processes involved in all past and present human activity such as social change, technological innovation, democratic participation, identity construction, knowledge production, and learning to teach oneself (Kincheloe, 2001a, p. 287).

In an economic context, to be prepared for work in the future, students need knowledge and skills in digital-age literacy that includes science, mathematics, technology, visual analysis, information analysis, cultural analysis, and global analysis. In addition, they need to be able to engage in inventive thinking that involve, curiosity, creativity, risk-taking, higher-order thinking, and the ability to manage complexity. Finally, they need knowledge and skill in technological fluency, communication, teamwork, leadership, problem solving, and creativity as well as effective communication that involves teaming, personal and social responsibility, and interactive communication skills (Thornburg, 2002, p. 59). In the early 1990s, two government reports that were focused on the workplace also reported that students not only needed preparation for future work in disciplinary areas such as reading, writing, and mathematics, but also in speaking and listening skills, problem-solving skills, creative thinking skills, knowing-how-to learn skills, collaboration and organizational skills, and personal management skills (Carnevale, Gainer, & Meltzer, 1990; Secretary's Commission on Achieving Necessary Skills, United States Department of Labor, 1991).

As indicated by these processes, standards of complexity are child centered in that knowledge is a means through which the child develops critical higher-order thinking skills that can be used to interrogate knowledge within the context of lived experience. In this way, what students learn and how they learn facilitates the development of habits that promote life-long learning. This child-centered curriculum is grounded in the assumption that all knowledge is a social and political construction, and, therefore, how power is arranged shapes not only the construction of knowledge but also each individual. To understand knowledge production in this context requires students to acquire and use higher-order thinking skills such as analysis, synthesis, evaluation, contextualization, and application. Students use these skills to form questions about knowledge *within* the framework of the curriculum but also *about* the curricular framework (Kincheloe, 2001a). This expanded context of learning "is flexible but rigorous, locally controlled but in touch with the knowledge production of various academic disciplines, concerned with content acquisition but also attentive to the multiple knowledge forms produced by individuals from diverse cultures, political/ideological perspectives, and paradigms" (Kincheloe, 2001c, p. 38). One view of education that directly relates curriculum to the local context is place-based education (Smith, 2000). Grounded in John Dewey's work at the University of Chicago Lab School, in the work of other early twentieth-century Progressive educators, and in the Foxfire Project in Georgia in the 1970s, students engage curriculum within the authentic context of their local community (Smith & Williams, 1999).

The comprehensive nature of a standards of complexity curriculum represents the sociological idea of totality in that social analysis always includes the uniqueness of individual experience as well as the larger social, economic, political, and cultural patterns that accompany all human activity. The totality of student learning within this context includes a critical context as expressed in these basic precepts that ground this kind of standards:

- higher-order thinking as a cognitive process of interpreting and analyzing rather than the commitment of a larger body of facts and formulae to memory
- the limitations of monocultural perspectives on the world
- the importance of examining how knowledge is produced and certified for curricular inclusion
- the ill-advisability of standardized education
- the need to confront racism, sexism, and class bias that distort student performance
- the importance of education in promoting democratic values and civic participation (Kincheloe, 2001c, p. 22).

These precepts disclose the ethics, justice, and democratic focus that pervade all standards of complexity. Like all types of standards, standards of complexity are a political project. In this case, this kind of standard attempts to reconnect information with meaning that is relevant to citizenship in a democratic society.

Unlike technical standards that represent the formalism of modernistic thinking, standards of complexity are postformal in the type of inquiry that they require of students. Postformal inquiry (Horn, 2001a; Kincheloe, 1998b; Kincheloe, Steinberg, & Hinchey, 1999) is an inquiry into the complexity of knowledge and social activity. In this postformal context, students examine the origins, context, and patterns of a phenomenon. Instead of viewing knowledge or human activity through a reductionist lens,

students learn to utilize diverse inquiry methods to uncover the deep and hidden patterns in which all knowledge is positioned. These patterns become apparent as students uncover and analyze the antecedents of a phenomenon and build a broad contextual knowledge base.

The emphasis that standards of complexity place on the holistic analysis of knowledge, the child-centered focus, and the acquisition of critical higher-order thinking skills can be seen in the values embedded within this curriculum proposed by Ivor Shor (1992). Shor promotes the value of a curriculum that:

- allows students' participation in their learning rather than being passive recipients of teacher-transmitted knowledge
- promotes the integration of positive emotions and cognition in the learning experience
- creates an educational experience in which the student actively poses and solves problems rather than sits passively as information is passed to the student
- utilizes themes and words from the student's daily life that situate the student's learning of any subject in the relevance and authenticity of that student's life
- fosters an awareness and understanding of the multicultural nature of the society in which the student lives
- utilizes a dialogical rather than adversarial type of conversation that allows the students to bind together in critically reflective thought and action
- desocializes the students in that they learn to question the social behaviors and experiences which surround them by critically examining their learned behavior
- facilitates the development of democratic ideals
- develops in the students an appreciation for and skill in utilizing research in decision making
- reviews the holistic nature of reality through interdisciplinary curriculum and instruction that creates in the students a willingness to take action in the promotion of democratic ideals.

The essential differences between the purposes of technical standards and standards of complexity are expressed in the following list that identifies an uncritical curricular position indicative of technical standards and a critical position indicative of standards of complexity:

- *Uncritical*: Society uses education to contribute to the maintenance and stability of the social, economic, and political order. *Critical*: Society uses education to contribute to the improvement, growth, and transformation of the social order (Astuto et al., 1994, p. 24).

- *Uncritical*: Schooling supports and promotes a common cultural heritage. *Critical*: schooling supports and promotes an understanding and appreciation of the diverse cultural traditions in American society (Astuto et al., 1994 p. 26).

- *Uncritical*: The test of the efficacy of an education system is its instrumental contribution to the goals of society. *Critical*: The test of the efficacy of an education system is the extent to which it meets the entitlement of all children to access the benefits of their society (Astuto et al., 1994 p. 10).

Standards of Complexity and Instruction

Many of the best practice elements that comprise instruction within standards of complexity systems may be found within technical standards systems. However, the essential difference in the use of instructional best practice in both systems lies within the different philosophies and purposes that ground these systems. In technical standards systems, best practices are instrumentally selected to situationally promote the performance standards and their assessment. Standards of complexity systems recognize that the consequences of how instruction occurs are just as important as the consequences on the students, teachers, and schools of the standards and assessments. Therefore, best practices are viewed as an integral part of the educational system, and any instruction other than best practice severely limits student learning and may have other deleterious consequences for the student.

Instruction in standards of complexity systems is tightly aligned with the purposes of standards of complexity. This system primarily focuses on the personal development of the students in relation to the development of the students' capacity to critically participate in American democracy. Secondary to this purpose is the use of education to meet the needs of the business community or any other special interest. In order to achieve this purpose, standards of complexity systems utilize a postformal

educational psychology as the basis for instruction. The following description of instructional methods used with standards of complexity characteristic of a postformal educational psychology.

Instructional Methods

In their instruction, teachers in a standards of complexity system are sensitive to student diversity because of the enormous impact that it has upon student learning. Student diversity involves such characteristics as gender, race, ethnicity, social class, and language. In addition, attention to diversity requires instructional sensitivity to multiple intelligences, cognitive styles, learning styles, and student affect or emotion. Also, multicultural diversity requires instruction that integrates examples and content from a variety of cultures and groups; facilitates the learning styles of students from different racial, cultural, and social class groups; empowers students from all demographic groups; attempts to reduce prejudicial thinking in students, and helps students understand the cultural assumptions attached to all content and the role of these assumptions in the construction of knowledge (Banks, 1994).

In order to facilitate learning in a standards of complexity system, instruction is interdisciplinary or parallel disciplinary. Interdisciplinary instruction (Clarke & Agne, 1997) requires teams of teachers from different content areas to integrate their specialized content through mutual planning and teaching. In parallel disciplinary teaching, the subjects may be taught individually with the teachers coordinating their curriculum and instruction to facilitate student understanding of the interrelatedness of all curriculum.

In standards of complexity systems, there is no pressure to cover designated content within a specific time frame because the instructional focus is on conceptual learning and higher-order thinking skills. In this way, students attain a deep understanding of knowledge and of how knowledge is constructed. The nature of an information society requires individuals to have the skill and knowledge that allows them to access, process, and evaluate information. These are essential skills in a time when there is an information explosion and rapid change. Memorization and recall of facts become inefficient uses of time when information quickly becomes obsolete. In a rapidly changing information environment, the focus of instruction is on the continual development of skills that can access, process, and critique information. Also, no knowledge or instructional techniques are privileged. All need to be critiqued.

In instruction based upon a postformal educational psychology, mastery learning and other applications of behavioral learning are reconceptualized. Instead of applying these techniques in a rigid manner that is tightly focused on the performance standards or the assessment, teachers use their professional intuition in knowing when to change the use of the behavioral technique in order to promote the primary purposes of standards of complexity systems. For instance, mastery learning may be used in peripheral remediation activities designed to overcome cognitive or skill deficits. However, as students engage these mastery learning remediation loops, teachers restructure the targeted content, utilize a variety of instructional techniques and assessments, and introduce a variety of materials. In addition, instead of a rote learning focus, this form of mastery learning is focused on student research involving content and questions that are embedded within situations that are authentically relevant to the students' experience. Also, reconceptualized mastery learning does not disrupt the student's relationship with other students. Students are not held back and curriculum is not displaced. Teachers accommodate both the social progress of students and the required skill development by utilizing opportunities in later activities to facilitate student growth in the required skills. In a Piagetian sense, teachers understand that students cognitively develop at different rates, and by providing ongoing interventions, this disparity in student cognitive development can be accommodated.

Other behavioral learning techniques, such as self-management, goal setting, behavioral modification, and positive reinforcement (Kazdin, 1989; Meichenbaum, 1979; Watson & Tharp, 1997), are appropriate techniques within a standards of complexity system. The final determination of whether a behavioral technique is being used appropriately depends upon whether it is building capacity in the student to be a self-directed, critically reflective life-long learner.

In standards of complexity systems, teachers are also critically grounded in cognitive psychology. **Metacognition**, or the

Metacognition

The act of process of knowing how we think.

awareness of one's cognitive activity, is an essential component of a standards of complexity system. The development of metacognitive awareness is an inherent aspect of all instruction. Standards of complexity systems teachers also utilize their awareness of Piagetian theory to facilitate student cognitive development. However, the constructivism of Piaget is enhanced through the addition of a critical awareness of the processes and consequences of knowledge construction. The social construction of knowledge and the importance of language in this process, as found in Vygotskian theory, guide the use of instructional techniques involving student-to-student interaction and teacher-to-student interaction. Instructional activities are informed and mediated by social cognitive learning theory that includes an awareness and application of observational learning, situated learning, inquiry and problem-based learning, group work and cooperative learning, dialogue and instructional conversation, and cognitive apprenticeships (Woolfolk, 2004).

Understanding that instruction and motivation are intertwined, standards of complexity systems teachers utilize a diversity of behavioral and humanistic approaches to motivate students. Because of the primary goal of personal development, the promotion of students' self-concept, self-esteem, and self-efficacy guides all instruction. Teachers design their instruction to work against learned helplessness while ensuring student learning and developing a sense of self-worth in their students. One important purpose in instruction that is attentive to student self-esteem is to help students develop the personal, intellectual, and social skills that not only promote their intellectual success but also helps them become happy, productive citizens of a democratic society (Neill & Medina, 1989).

Instruction that utilizes post-formal educational psychology seldom contains teacher-directed transmission of knowledge in programmed instruction formats. Instructional activities for all students focus on student construction of knowledge through discovery and the fostering of student creativity. This type of instruction seldom employs best practice in a conditional and contrived manner but strives to instill the knowledge and critique of best practice in students so that they will continue to utilize the best learning practices in their experience outside of the classroom. Helping students expand their understanding of knowledge con-

Critical reflection

When individuals reflect upon the social justice consequences of their actions.

struction enhances the students' ability to apply knowledge acquired in the classroom to the rest of their life experiences. This is accomplished by having students **critically reflect** on knowledge and inquiry on three levels. Reflection on knowledge and inquiry-*for*-practice involves student understanding of how knowledge is acquired by engaging in research in a scholarly manner. Reflection on knowledge and inquiry-*in*-practice involves the understanding that students gain by critically reflecting on the processes that they use while engaging in research. Reflection on knowledge and inquiry-*of*-practice involves student reflection on the knowledge gained through individual and collective inquiry (Cochran-Smith & Lytle, 1999).

Instructional Technology

The use of instructional technology in standards of complexity systems is focused on the support of instructional activities; however, once again the purpose behind standards of complexity informs and mediates the use of technology. The goals of student personal growth and participation in American democracy expand the concept of instructional technology from uncontested and neutral purveyors of information to resources that are critiqued through the use of higher-order thinking skills. In standards of complexity classrooms, all the information provided by textbooks, supplemental materials, computer technology, videos, primary and secondary sources, and teacher and student-constructed materials are critiqued to uncover the assumptions, representations, and consequences of the way the resources are organized in the content that is presented by these materials.

All instructional technology is used within a student research context. No resources are privileged in that they are believed to provide a complete representation of their subject. All resources are viewed as locations in which the information provided by the resource may represent only one interpretation of the information or may only present the information within a specific context. Students engaged in the research process will learn to access, process, and evaluate information about a specific topic from multiple sources, and critique the multiple interpretations of knowledge provided by the sources.

The most important resources in standards of complexity learning environments will be those constructed by the teacher and the students. Whether audio-visual representations of information, readings, charts, graphs, surveys, interviews, role-playing scenarios, websites, or newsletters, the act of constructing these resources and the proper use of their production technologies support student personal growth and the skills that are essential for critical and effective participation in American democracy. Additionally, community resources and primary sources also support the goals of personal growth and democratic participation. With the increasing importance of the Internet as a primary information source, students need to learn how to access, process, and evaluate this information for its accuracy, validity, and ideological intent. Since media representations of information greatly impact how we interpret the past, present, and future, students need to apply the same thought processes to this source of information.

Of secondary importance are textbooks, supplemental materials, and other commercially prepared instructional materials. When these materials are used, students need to develop the skills to identify and critique the hidden assumptions conveyed by the text's representation of the information. By engaging a diversity of instructional resources, students can identify and analyze the various contexts that are or are not provided by each source. Through a postformal analysis of all resources, students will uncover the origins of the various positions and develop a broad contextual knowledge of the subject. From this research into the origins and context of the subject under study, students will discern larger patterns within which the subject is nested and therefore gain a broader and deeper knowledge of the subject. Student research that employs a diversity of resources and technologies enables students to experience the diversity of positions that are held about all knowledge.

The Instructional Schedule

Standards of complexity can guide instruction that is organized into the previously described traditional 45-minute blocks or longer class periods as found in block-scheduling systems. In a fully implemented standards of complexity systems, student assessment is ongoing and multiple in nature and therefore has little effect on the instructional schedule. Flexible schedules allow for a greater degree of instructional flexibility. Flexible schedules better accommodate teacher spontaneity in instruction, the use of community resources, activities that require longer periods of continuous instruction, and conferencing and remediation activities.

The Role of the Teacher

Like all aspects of a standards of complexity system, the instructional role of the teacher is defined in such a way as to promote the purposes of student growth and the development of a critical democratic citizenry. This purpose is succinctly expressed in the statement that teachers who operate in a standards of complexity system are "agents of democracy who understand the relationship between learning and the future existence of a democratic state" (Kincheloe, 2001a, p. 286). Individuals who perform the role of teacher in standards of complexity systems are an inherently different type of teacher than those in a technical standards system. Quite different terms are used to describe their role, such as transformative intellectuals (Giroux, 1988, 1993), scholar-teachers (Kincheloe, 2001a), scholar-practitioners (Bentz, 2002; Jenlink, 2002; Muth, 2002), and transformational learners (Mezirow, 2000; Saavedra, 1995). All of these terms are similar in that they view teachers as reflective, empowered professionals who utilize theory and practice to transform learning into an effective, empowering, and liberating activity. This teacher role can be understood within the context of their decision-making capacity and their position within the school hierarchy, their professional expertise, how their professional effectiveness is evaluated, and the nature of their motivation.

Since teachers are the closest professionals to the students, they are entrusted with the ability to make decisions about curriculum, instruction, and assessment within the guidelines established by the **school community.** Meeting student needs and providing effective instruction are accomplished through continuous teacher reflection and subsequent teacher action based upon the reflection. Standards of complexity systems recognize the changing context of the learning process and require teachers to accommodate these changes through changes in their instruction. Unlike the teacher-proof instruction that characterizes technical

School community

In relation to a specific school district, all of the individuals who are affected by that local school district. The term can be broadened to include a region, state, or the nation.

standards systems, teachers are not micro-managed but empowered professionals who are responsible for the learning process. Instead of being viewed as variables that need to be controlled, teachers are members of leadership teams, inquiry groups, professional development, and other capacity-building activities (Muth, 2002, pp. 23–24). Their participation in these activities is not of a contrived and limited nature but participation in policy decision-making. This type of professional participation blurs the traditional boundaries between teacher and administration. Schools that are not organized in a traditional hierarchical structure are flatter organizations because of the involvement of teachers in activities that are traditionally reserved for administration and school board.

In order to function in this expanded professional role, the professional expertise of teachers is defined quite differently from their roles within a technical standards system. The complexity of their role, which requires an equally complex level of expertise, is apparent in this description of the role of a scholar-teacher. "These scholar-teachers treat students as active agents, render knowledge problematic, utilize dialogical methods of teaching, and seek to make learning a process where self-understanding, self-direction, and learning to teach oneself are possible" (Kincheloe, 2001a, p. 286). What is the level of professional expertise required of a teacher to accomplish this instructional task?

Teachers need not only to be knowledgeable of their content specialty but also knowledgeable in the other disciplines. Teachers who have knowledge of all disciplines are able to facilitate student development of a broad contextual knowledge base that connects different disciplines and allows the student to see patterns of knowledge that cross disciplinary boundaries. Besides acquiring this broad interdisciplinary knowledge base, teachers also acquire the critical skills necessary to critique disciplinary knowledge in order to uncover its effects on identity construction, knowledge production, learning to teach oneself, democratic participation, technological innovation, and social change (Kincheloe, 2001, p. 286).

This critique is accomplished through teacher inquiry into how one perceives and acquires knowledge. As previously described within the context of student instructional activity, teachers also engage in the three levels of knowledge and inquiry identified by Cochran-Smith and Lytle (2002) and Jenlink (1999). The ability of teachers to inquire into knowledge is essential within a standards of complexity system not only because this type of inquiry is expected of students, but it also is the core activity of all professional development.

Besides of their acquisition of broad disciplinary knowledge, teachers are grounded in the pedagogical best practices found in a postformal educational psychology. Through their use of best practice and through a constant critical reflection on their situational effectiveness, teachers selectively use a variety of pedagogical tools as needed to promote effective teaching and learning. The situational use of different pedagogical techniques is possible because, as scholar-practitioners, teachers allow theory to mediate and inform their practice and their practice to inform their use of theory. Instead of being technicians who merely implement the theory-based practice constructed by outside experts, these teachers dynamically construct theory and practice as determined by their critical reflection on their teaching and on the education needs of their students.

An additional factor that contributes to a critical and effective pedagogy is the teacher's understanding and use of the different types of conversation that occur in the learning environment. Four basic types of conversation that are a part of all human activity are discussion, dialectical, dialogue, and design (Jenlink & Carr, 1996). Discussion and dialectical conversation are conflictual types in that the purpose of both is to "win" the conversation. Dialogue and design are forms of collegial conversation in that their purpose is to promote understanding of divergent viewpoints. In teacher-directed technical standards systems, conflictual conversation is the norm with dialogue occurring in a tightly controlled manner. This type of conversation occurs whenever "right" answers drive the instruction. Teacher positions need to be defended, and opposing student positions need to be defeated. In a standards of complexity system, teachers need to be able to effectively engage in all types of conversation and have the ability to facilitate dialogic conversation that allows all views to be presented and critiqued in an egalitarian manner. Since conversation is ubiquitous in all learning activity, teachers need to be aware of the types of conversation

and their consequences.

Utilizing their broad disciplinary knowledge and pedagogical best practices, teachers are mindful scholar-practitioners who are aware of the economic, political, social, cultural, and ecological situations in which their practice is occurring (Bentz, 2002, p. 19). This awareness is transferred to their students who can examine knowledge within the political, economic, social, cultural, and ethical context in which all knowledge resides.

A final aspect of the role of teachers in a standards of complexity system is that these teachers must be bricoleurs (Crotty, 1998; Denzin and Lincoln, 1994; Jenlink, 2002; Kincheloe, 1998a; Levi-Strauss, 1966). The teacher-as-bricoleur is the teacher who employs a wide range of methodological tools in the attempt to understand a phenomenon. Whether the focus is on a specific pedagogical technique, content, or student learning, the teacher-as-bricoleur uses a diversity of information collection methods and epistemological philosophies to uncover the deep and hidden aspects of the phenomenon.

How is the effectiveness of a teacher such as this evaluated? Unlike technical standards systems that focus teacher effectiveness solely on student test performance, standards of complexity systems take a holistic view of teacher assessment. The assessment of teacher effectiveness occurs within the same philosophical framework used in student assessment. The essential point in using this framework is that an accurate picture of a teacher's effectiveness cannot be obtained through the use of a single assessment. Since a single assessment provides a decontextualized snapshot of teacher effectiveness, it cannot capture the complexity of the teacher's role. Therefore, like student assessment in standards of complexity systems, multiple authentic assessments are used. These can include peer assessment, self-assessment, student assessment, parent assessment, and formal administrative assessment. Also, professional portfolios can be structured to reflect all of the dimensions of teacher activity. The portfolios can be running records of yearlong teacher activity, or showcase portfolios. Portfolios can be aligned with the teacher's yearly goals. Using a variety of multiple assessments guarantees a more comprehensive picture of teacher activity, and the conclusions that are made are well documented. In addition, this type of evidence-based assessment is focused on the professional growth of the

teacher, as well as on a determination of teacher effectiveness at a specific point in time.

As in the other aspects of a teacher's role, motivation in a standards of complexity system is of a different nature. As described, teachers in this system are self-directed and reflective professionals. Teachers can be extrinsically motivated through the assessment process. However, the greater motivation is the intrinsic motivation that is the by-product of empowerment. Empowered teachers are vested in student learning quite differently from the disempowered technicians of the technical standards systems. The degree of student learning that occurs is a reflection upon the practice that *they choose* to use, not upon externally imposed practice. In this case, there is a direct relationship between how they taught and how the students achieved. In technical standards systems, teachers can disassociate themselves from student learning and blame the externally imposed practices for poor student learning. Standards of complexity systems demand a greater degree of professional accountability than technical systems because all aspects of the teacher's professional experience are being effectively evaluated, and the teacher is an active participant in this process.

Professionalism and Professional Development

In standards of complexity systems, the purpose of professional development is to develop professionals who are life-long learners, grow as professionals, and ensure student achievement of the standards of complexity. As in all educational systems, professional development occurs within and outside of the school, and is viewed as a normal and ongoing activity in the professional lives of teachers. Professional development within standards of complexity systems is inherently more demanding in that teachers are not constrained to content specialties or simplistic instructional techniques. Instead, teachers must continuously develop their capacity as critically aware scholars and practitioners, not only in relation to one discipline or grade level, but also as educational generalists who understand the broad context of curriculum that includes the integration of all subjects. In addition, they must develop their capacity to extend their critical awareness beyond the school to include all other cultural, economic, political, and social aspects that impact education.

In standards of complexity systems, professional development within the school is authentic and relevant to teachers. This is guaranteed by the participation of teachers in determining the content and structure of the development activity. In their analysis of school needs, teachers and administrators collectively organize professional development activities. In this process, the main focus of professional development activity arises out of teacher research involving curriculum and instruction. Teachers are viewed as self-directed reflective professionals who engage in schoolwide inquiry that becomes the basis for school reform. As scholar-practitioner researchers, teachers not only engage in individual research but also in collaborative research with other teachers, universities, and educational specialists. Professional development also includes developing teacher research skills, grounding teacher practice in theory, developing the teachers' ability to reflect upon their practice and inform their practice with theory, and the generation of theory that is shaped by reflection upon practice. In this way, teachers are engaged in "a theory of transformative learning [that] sees learning as a continuous, life-long process by which learners are constantly making meaning within the realities of their everyday lives" (Anderson & Saavedra, 2002, p. 23).

Professional development also occurs outside of the school as teachers pursue advanced degrees and additional certifications. In addition, teachers may encounter best practice if their schools are partners with universities. Professional development schools not only help preservice teachers develop instructional practices based on best practice theory but also provide professional development opportunities for all teachers within the participating school district.

The Role of the Administration and the School Board

How the roles of school administration, school boards, teachers, and students are reconceived is critical if schools are to effectively meet the diverse and, in some cases, incompatible goals placed upon them by competing interests in society. At the same time, schools are asked to provide education that is representative of purposes and services that are often incompatible with the time and money allocated for public education. For instance, schools are to provide education that is at the same time equitable and excellent within the constraints of increasedclass size, reduced and inequitably distributed funding of public schools, and increasing control by special interests external to the school. They are asked to provide a plethora of academic, social, mental, and physical health services and to do so in a quality way. Also, they are asked to guarantee student attainment of basic skills and higher-order thinking when the reality of standardized testing mandates demand teaching to the informational fragments contained within these tests.

Just as teachers function in complex intertwined multidimensional roles as instructors of academic knowledge, counselors in meeting student needs, and supervisors of their defined work environment, administrator roles are equally complex. Administrators must balance their competing roles that deal with fiscal, personnel, public relations, legal, political, and instructional leadership responsibilities. All of these responsibilities must be met in an environment in which their autonomy and control are being restricted. To meet their responsibilities in an ethical and moral way requires a redefinition of the role of the administrator. This reconceptualization of the role is critical because the relationship between administrators and teachers is reproduced in the relationship between teachers and students. If the purpose of public education is to ensure the personal growth of students and to construct a democratically literate, participatory, and responsive citizenry, then egalitarian organizations, structures, and personal relationships between administrators and teachers need to guide the operation of the educational system.

For this to occur, administrative leadership styles need to be consistent with the philosophy that is the foundation of standards of complexity. Unlike the rigid organizational leadership styles of business-oriented technical standards systems that create cellular structures resulting in stakeholder isolation, collegial and egalitarian styles that emphasize blurred stakeholder boundaries need to be established. These flatter hierarchies, which emphasize informal relationships, more effectively utilize the contributions of all stakeholders in meeting the multiple and divergent demands placed upon public schools. Some scholars argue that the essential problem with top-down controlled bureaucracies is how autonomy and control are organized within the hierarchy (Shedd

& Bacharach, 1991). This view maintains that "the problems now besetting America's systems of public education require more discretion *and* more control, more flexibility *and* more direction, more room for professional judgment *and* more ways of ensuring accountability" (Shedd & Bacharach, 1991, p. 5). In standards of complexity systems, this is accomplished through the empowerment of all stakeholders and through the development of collegial professional relationships that are unlike the adversarial relationships of traditional educational systems. This perspective recognizes that the complexity of the demands placed on the public schools can only be resolved through a concomitant relational complexity among administrators, teachers, and students. Instead of focusing on one's own responsibilities within one's own level, the creativity, knowledge, skill, and motivation of all individuals in the system are directed at making the *whole* system work.

A leadership style espoused by Thomas Sergiovanni (1992, 1994) is an example of a style that can tap this collective potential for fostering effective and egalitarian schools. Sergiovanni proposes that by constructing a covenant of shared values, administrators and teachers can join in a common cause that transforms a school into an educational community focused on promoting those values. Sergiovanni argues that through the moral leadership and stewardship of the educational leader, administrators and teachers can collegially build just and caring school communities that effectively meet the societal demands placed on them. A similar view of schools as professional learning communities proposes the development of shared missions, visions, and values through collective and collaborative inquiry that is committed to continuous improvement through innovation and experimentation (Dufour & Eaker, 1998).

The type of community proposed by Sergiovanni is like the Gemeinschaft community identified in the late 1880s by Ferdinand Tönnies (1887/1957), in which community is based on a shared vision or oneness—a community in which all share a common identity and a concern for other members of the community. In contrast to gemeinschaft community, Tönnies identified another perspective on community—Gesellschaft. Gesellschaft is based on contractual arrangements, and the relationships between individuals are impersonal and contrived.

Sergiovanni (1994) maintains that traditional American school-ing is indicative of a Gesellschaft mentality in that we have become conditioned "to adopt an impersonal, bureaucratic, pro-fessional, managerial, and technical language" (p. 29). The signif-icance of what Sergiovanni writes is that in Gesellschaft-type communities, it is difficult to deviate from the definitions of participation, authority, and empowerment that are inherent to this type of community. Standards of complexity require a move from Gesellchaft societies promoted by technical standards sys-tems, to the formation of Gemeinschaft communities. Not only does the potential to meet the demands placed on the school increase, but also the idea of Gemeinschaft community is better aligned with the nature of a democratic society. To build this type of community requires school boards to empower administrators and teachers to reconceptualize their roles and, subsequently, the organization of the school.

The Role of the Parents, the Community, and the Students

As in the case of administrators and teachers, standards of complexity systems require a reconceptualization of the roles of parents, students, and the community. These stakeholders are not viewed as variables whose function is solely to facilitate stu-dent achievement of technical standards. Instead, these stake-holders are directly involved in the determination and promotion of the shared values that accommodate *all* of the social and cul-tural difference that is part of the community. The tension between the professionalism of the school and community involvement in the school (Bauch & Goldring, 1998; Crowson, 1998; Mawhinney, 1998; Ogawa, 1998) is mediated by the for-mation of professional and personal relationships between the members of the school and the community. Starting with com-munity participation in the determination of the guiding shared values, bridges are constructed that allow for authentic commu-nity participation, and for the education of the community in the complexities of educational leadership, organization, teaching, and learning. Through these bridges, educators and community mem-bers identify their responsibilities for the promotion of the shared values and establish networks that facilitate their implementation. For instance, focus group data from Public Agenda surveys

(Johnson, 2003; Public Agenda, 2003) indicate that the majority of the public want standards and accountability reforms; however, they do not believe that one test should be the basis for student promotion. In a standards of complexity environment, educators and parents would work together to establish just, caring, and equitable standards and accountability systems for all students.

Since standards of complexity systems view educational communities as comprised of interrelated and interconnected subsystems, the needs of the school and those of the community are connected. Because of this interconnection, administrators and teachers must become critical participants within the community activity. Standards of complexity systems require educators to become cultural workers and promote egalitarian and participatory democracy in the community by becoming political agents in the resolution of community issues (Giroux, 1996; Greene, 1988). By taking critical action in the community, authentic bridges are constructed that allow both educators and community members to deeply understand each other's needs. This type of political activity is authentic because it goes beyond the contrived and superficial back-to-school nights and school district newsletters in fostering equitable and caring relationships between the school and the community. In this kind of professional activity by the educators, the focus of the school is not on technical standards that are largely irrelevant to the school and community but on the realization that the welfare of the school and the community is realized through caring and democratic participation by all members of the school community.

In standards of complexity systems, students take on a different role than in technical standards systems. Instead of being disempowered passive recipients of externally imposed knowledge, students assume the role of **students-as-researchers** (Kincheloe & Steinberg, 1998). As empowered learners guided by the instructional practices of a reconceptualized educational psychology, students learn to critically investigate knowledge and construct knowledge that is relevant to their personal growth and future participants in American democracy. In a study of high-performing Hispanic schools, the schools encouraged students to be empowered participants in the learning process by providing opportu-

Students-as-researchers

Students are empowered to uncover the social, political, and pedagogical aspects of schooling that shape their consciousness.

nities for experimentation, discovery, and problem solving (Reyes, Scribner, & Scribner, 1999). As educators and community members join in promoting education and solving community problems, students participate in these activities. One outcome is that students realize that their responsibility to learn extends beyond realization of their personal goals to include service to the community in which they reside. In this type of educational context, students are engaged in authentic and socially relevant moral development.

In 1991, in order to inform the America 2000 initiative, Lynn Martin, the Secretary of Labor formed a commission to investigate the changes in the world of work and the implications of those changes for learning. The Secretary's Commission on Achieving Necessary Skills (SCANS), which consisted of 30 members of whom six were educators, found that students needed to perform a role as learner that was quite different from the role required by technical standards systems. SCANS reported that schools needed to create learning opportunities in which students would actively construct knowledge for themselves, engage in cooperative problem solving, learn skills in the context of real problems, and learn to think (Secretary's Commission on Achieving Necessary Skills, United States Department of Labor, 1991, p. 22). SCANS considered this student role as a critical component in achieving Goal Number Five of the six National Goals of America 2000.

Standards of Complexity and Assessment

Because of their inherent focus on the complexity of human experience, standards of complexity systems require multiple assessments. Reliance on one test or one type of assessment cannot capture the complexity of the learning process. The use of both holistic and analytical assessment facilitates the formative and summative assessment that leads to the broad understandings and specific determinations of all aspects of student achievement. Holistic assessment can include all types of portfolio-based assessment, performance exams, proficiency exit standards, exhibitions, parent conferences, school report cards, scoring rubrics, holistic scoring, numerical rating scales, and peer and self-assessments. Analytical assessment in the form of objective class-

room tests, essay tests, and standardized tests can be used for diagnostic and evaluative purposes. However, the guiding principle in the assessment of standards of complexity is the use of multiple assessment techniques in order to capture the full context of student learning, which includes student cognition, affect, and ability. Assessment in this system recognizes the diversity in:

- Student cognitive styles of learning (i.e., the different ways that students perceive and organize information),
- Learning styles (i.e., the different ways that students approach studying and learning),
- Ethnic and racial differences in student learning,
- The learning of exceptional and disabled children,
- The learning of children for whom English is the second language,
- The different ways in which society's beliefs about males and females affect how they process information and their development of self-esteem as learners.

In pursuit of the goal of developing life-long learners, the assessment of standards of complexity promotes self-directed learning and conceptual understanding of knowledge in the context of a student's own life experiences. In addition, students are required to reflect on what they learned and on the learning processes that they used. Also, since students are viewed as researchers, assessment must accommodate this component of life-long learning. To promote critical life-long learners, there needs to be assessment flexibility that facilitates the students' own formative and summative assessment of their focus on the consequences of their learning in relation to the issues of social justice, caring, and democratic participation.

The following characteristics of assessment in standards of complexity systems are based upon the general principles of alternative assessment as proposed by Peterson and Neill (2001):

- Support improved learning by providing feedback for the improvement of student learning.
- Help teachers teach better by providing instructional feedback.
- Integrate assessment with the curriculum and instruction.
- Assessments are classroom based in that they are based on classroom work done by students over time.

- Use a variety of measures, not a single assessment, and include individual and schoolwide data.
- Promote positive collaboration through the involvement of educators, parents, and the broader community in the assessment process.
- Don't straightjacket the curriculum in that assessment promotes flexibility for curriculum and instruction to meet student needs in the learning process. (p. 984)

In addition, assessment in standards of complexity systems is focused on assessment *for* learning rather than on assessment *of* learning (Stiggins, 2002). In this case, the use of assessment *for* learning has a diagnostic function that occurs within the classroom context and is used to continuously construct authentic and effective instructional practice that promotes positive student growth.

Challenges in the Use of Alternative Assessment

The promotion of outcomes-based education in the 1990s, which utilized alternative assessments, is a case study in the challenges faced by the proponents of this assessment philosophy. In states that attempted to implement outcomes-based learning, students were required to demonstrate their achievement of the standards through the use of non-traditional assessment. One commonly used assessment was a portfolio that contained activities assessed by rubrics. Some schools instituted portfolio systems that included yearly portfolios that would follow students through to graduation. These portfolios were focused either solely on content or a mix of content and basic skills that were relevant to each subject area. Some portfolios that were organized around these basic or megaskills included categories such as writen communication, oral communication, reading, use of technology, critical thinking, life skills, collaborative learning, and self-awareness. The assumption was that these categories represented the skills that were necessary for vocational and academic success and for the development of life-long learners. In addition, some academic areas used portfolios in which organizing categories were based on content and skill standards developed by their respective professional organizations.

Also included in many outcome-based education initiatives

was the use of project-based learning and assessment. Generally, along the lines of the exhibitions utilized in Sizer's (1984, 1992, 1996) Coalition of Essential Schools, students would demonstrate their ability to effectively synthesize these skills in completing a sizable interdisciplinary project that would be a requirement for promotion to a higher grade or for graduation. In many cases, these projects involved the student's interaction with a community issue or problem. In addition, other holistic and analytical assessments were used in conjunction with the portfolios and projects in this deep and broad assessment of student achievement.

Unfortunately in many schools, these multiple assessments fell out of favor with the political demise of outcome-based education. An analysis of that resistance to this assessment philosophy can be used to identify the challenges of using this assessment philosophy in the current climate of standards and accountability. Since most individuals never experienced this type of assessment, all of the stakeholders in the educational community need to learn about the benefits and disadvantages of this type in relation to those of traditional assessment. This poses a second challenge relating to the time that would be needed to build support for alternative assessment. Time is problematic because the public is politically conditioned to believe in the viability of educational quick fixes. Time is also a problem because, like the public, most educators have little experience with alternative assessment beyond the theory that they encountered in their teacher preparation courses. Therefore, time would have to be provided for educators to learn about these assessments within the classroom context and then to reach consensus concerning their use. A related problem involves the additional work that is required to develop the instructional and assessment capacity to implement such a system. However, this work is secondary to the development of the teachers' belief in the critical foundations of this type of assessment. To commit to alternative assessment requires a belief that is informed by an analysis of the current system, in the idea that the purpose of assessment is to provide effective, relevant, authentic, and equitable teaching and learning. Also another important consideration is whether educators, parents, and community members will become part of the political process that guides the development of educational policy. Political participation on the local,

state, and national level would be necessary in order to provide a secure base of support for alternative assessment.

Issues of Validity and Reliability

Multiple and authentic assessment is inherently valid in that it measures what it intend to measure. In standards of complexity systems, the primary purposes of assessment are to promote personal growth in the student and student participation in American democracy. Effective vocational and academic preparation is an inherent by-product of personal growth. The inclusive and holistic nature of multiple and authentic assessment provides a comprehensive and detailed understanding of student learning, not only for a teacher's assessment of the learning but also for the students' assessment of their own learning. A more important form of validity in standards of complexity systems is catalytic validity (Lather, 1991). A learning process that is catalytically valid is one that enables students to not only understand the world through their studies but also enables them to take action and transform the world. In this sense, if learning is valid, then self-understanding, self-direction, and democratic participation are promoted in the students. In standards of complexity systems, students show personal growth in their ability to better understand the complexities of life through their own self-reflection. In this case, assessment is transformed from an externally imposed system of rewards and punishments to an activity perceived by students to be a naturally occurring and self-enhancing part of the learning process.

The use of multiple assessments also meets the reliability requirement of assessment. Through the diagnostic use of norm-referenced standardized tests, schools can assess their student performance in relation to state and national norms. In addition, the use of multiple assessments guarantees consistency in determining student performance, not through the use of a statistical measure but through the quantity and diversity of the documentation that is provided. Through authentic assessment, the local uniqueness of student learning can be used to inform and mediate learning in other places.

Equity and Ethics

In standards of complexity systems, the issues of equity and ethics are not viewed as factors that have to be considered because the demands of certain types of instruction and assessment may cause inequitable and unethical outcomes. Instead, the essential critical purposes of standards of complexity, that guide curriculum, instruction, and assessment constantly promote equitable education and ethical educator behavior. Because of the student-centered focus and the continual critical reflection on educational practice and stakeholder empowerment, considerations of equity and ethics naturally occur throughout the learning process. How certain individuals may gain advantage or disadvantage in the assessment process quickly becomes apparent as teachers, students, and parents critically reflect upon the assessment consequences. Consequences such as high dropout rates are not viewed as naturally occurring phenomena that will eventually be reduced through more regimentation but as evidence of the failure of some aspect of instruction and assessment. The egalitarian nature of standards of complexity systems in the valuation of difference and diversity requires that assessment cannot marginalize or oppress. Instead assessment must facilitate student achievement without denigrating the diverse cultural backgrounds of students and must assist students of all socioeconomic levels in the maximization of the cultural capital that will allow them to grow as individuals and to critically participate in American democracy. In addition, standards of complexity systems recognize the critical importance of "early-childhood education programs, when they are taught in small classes by skilled and committed teachers, and when they are given assessments linked to appropriate and immediate responses" (Orfield & Wald, 2000, p. 75). In this way, a solid foundation is constructed for equitable and effective future learning.

As in technical standards systems, instruction and assessment are also dynamically connected in this system. However, unlike the propensity to teach to the test in standardized testing situations, the goal of instruction in standards of complexity systems is to promote the standards and their purpose, not to accommodate the assessment. The use of multiple assessments guarantees the emphasis on student achievement of the standards, not student achievement on one high-stakes test. Accountability to the standards is maintained in an equitable and ethical manner because each assessment provides a different perspective on instructional practice, how the standards are represented by that practice, and on how well the students performed in relation to the standards. Once again, concerns about equity and ethics naturally arise out of the continuous stakeholder reflection on instruction and assessment in relation to the purpose and content of the standards.

Student Motivation and Emotional Response

Because students are empowered self-directed learners in standards of complexity systems, student learning is motivated by their participation in the instructional process, not by extrinsic rewards and punishments associated with a standardized test. In this type of system, the boundaries between formative and summative assessment are blurred. Diagnosis and evaluation occur with each assessment. The intent of all assessment is to promote student growth and success. Students may experience anxiety as a natural part of the learning process but not to the potentially debilitating degree associated with standardized tests. This anxiety is allayed in a large part because all assessment is viewed as essential feedback in the growth process. Failure on an assessment carries no life-altering outcomes but is posed as a feedback mechanism in the pursuit of excellence. The negative effects of failure are muted because each assessment clearly identifies student growth and student progress in meeting the standards.

The use of rubrics in determining mastery of basic skills and portfolios in determining growth over time acts as a scaffold that promotes student achievement. Also, because students are viewed as co-constructors of their learning, they consider assessment as a positive and integral part of the learning process. Instead of experiencing feelings of shame, guilt, and helplessness through an emphasis on failure, students are positively reinforced in all assessments by the focus on what they achieved. This focus on the positive and the accumulating evidence of their growth and success facilitates their further investment in the learning process. Instead of representing fear and dread, multiple and authentic assessment systems represent opportunities for students to actualize their potential. Also in this positive motivational and emo-

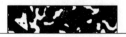

tional climate, the use of standardized tests as diagnostic tools rather than ranking and sorting mechanisms, carries less psychic trauma.

The tendency of standardized test environments toward the disaggregation of test results into demographic groups positions marginalized children in a negative way. Their difference is represented as a negative that must be overcome for the good of the school. In standards of complexity systems, student ethnic and racial diversity is valued as a positive contribution to the learning community. Cultural differences are recognized as enhancements to the learning process. The burden of the socioeconomic disadvantage suffered by some children is not placed upon the individual child but shouldered by the whole learning community as it strives to offset the deleterious effects of the child's low socioeconomic status. This positive recognition of diversity and difference is evident in the student-centered and student growth focus that is inherent in multiple and authentic assessments.

As critically informed transformative intellectuals, scholar-teachers, or scholar-practitioners, educators recognize the social conditions (such as funding, poverty, and abuse) that impact their students' learning and take action within and outside of the school to confront these social problems. This recognition of the social context that underlies poor student achievement mediates the assessment process. The act of student assessment is extended from only assessing student achievement of the standards to include the identification of the larger and more important factors that impact student achievement. This broader definition of assessment provides invaluable feedback that can be used to better promote student success. In learning environments characterized by curriculum, instruction, and assessment that are just and caring, students replace dread with joy and become intrinsically rather than extrinsically motivated learners.

Glossary

Critical reflection—when individuals reflect upon the social justice consequences of their actions.

Metacognition—The act of process of knowing how we think.

School community—in relation to a specific school district, all of the individuals who are affected by that local school district. The term can be broadened to include a region, state, or the nation.

Students-as-researchers—Students are empowered to uncover the social, political, and pedagogical aspects of schooling that shape their consciousness.

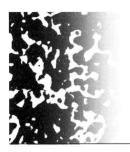

CHAPTER FIVE

Conclusion

In conclusion, it is evident that the debate over standards and accountability is a heated one that will only grow more contentious as an increasing number of students, parents, and educators experience the implications and consequences of the current reform. The *Standards Primer* has explored the foundations and practice of two essentially different views on this issue. From this exploration, certain conclusions can be drawn and issues raised.

One conclusion is that technical standards and standards of complexity represent very different educational philosophies and purposes. As discussed, technical standards are philosophically grounded in the realism of modern thinking. Knowledge is organized into separate disciplines that are incrementally taught in a linear sequence and, in most cases, objectively assessed by a standardized test. Accountability is primarily focused on the individual who is expected to have the *will* to achieve. Instruction is standards focused and to a large degree is transmissional in nature. Authority over knowledge, teaching, and learning resides in the expert.

In contrast, standards of complexity are philosophically grounded in the pragmatism, skepticism, and criticality of postmodern thinking. Knowledge is viewed holistically and presented in an interdisciplinary context. Learning is viewed as an ongoing process in which all participants individually and socially construct meaning. In addition, learning is structured to facilitate problem solving through the use of higher-order thinking that is both logical in the use of deduction and induction and creative in the reliance on intuition to arrive at solutions by finding new connections between ideas. Assessment is multiple and authentic. Accountability is seen as a systemwide phenomenon that is individual and collective in nature. Authority over knowledge, teaching, and learning is shared among all stakeholders in the educational system. The implication of this essential difference between these two views on standards is that each holds quite different consequences for all educational stakeholders, their communities, and how individuals participate in American democracy.

Another conclusion is that the debate over standards and accountability is inherently a political debate. The political values of reactionaries, conservatives, liberals, and radicals are manifested in the various positions that are taken on this educational reform. The Right and the Left attempt to promote their agendas on related educational issues such as multiculturalism, school choice, educational funding, character education, and the privatization of public schools. These ideological interests attempt to institute their ideas by controlling the definition, organization, and implementation of standards and accountability reforms. An important implication of this political activity involves the competing goals of constructing a society that is defined by a common culture or one that is pluralistic in its valuation of diversity and difference. The important question that is often lost in this intense political activity is how we can balance the need for cultural commonality with the inclusion of the diversity and difference that leads to an enriched and vibrant culture.

In addition, the business sector strenuously lobbies for a standards and accountability reform that promotes their economic interests. Instructional philosophies, methods, and techniques common to the business sector are applied to education in the hope that they will foster an educational system that will be effective and efficient in promoting the interests of this sector. In addition, public education represents an enormous outlay of money that can flow to the business sector through the privatization of schools and by the ability of businesses to provide educational resources and training. Also, the business sector recognizes the value of the students as consumers and future workers and attempts to influence their development in these roles. With service workers representing the largest occupational need for the business community, businesses attempt to pass along the cost of basic skills training to the public schools (Berliner & Biddle, 1996; Bracey, 2002; Sacks, 1999).

Besides these general conclusions, certain issues are raised through an understanding of the complexity of standards and accountability reform. One issue that is raised by the intense focus on accountability is that of trust. The Bracey Reports that annually appear in the Phi Delta Kappan journal indicate that most Americans are satisfied with the educational experience that is provided by their local educators. However, paradoxically, these same individuals have a much lower opinion of education in other places. How can the same individuals trust their local educators but not trust others to be equally accountable for effective education? Bracey, among others, has speculated that when the public is personally involved with their schools and educators, they have the necessary information to make informed decisions about educational accountability and school effectiveness. However, the information that they use to pass judgment on other schools and educators is primarily derived from political groups and the media representations of education, educators, and different types of students. Numerous scholars who engage in cultural pedagogy report **patterns of representation** in movies, television, and print media that represent education, educators, and certain types of students in negative stereotypical ways. These scholars further argue that these representations are due to the political activity of various interests that is designed to promote their ideological and economic agendas.

Patterns of representation

One group's repetitious presentation of how another group is defined in attempt to control that group.

In relation to the issue of accountability, many individuals argue that the public needs to become critically aware of these representations and their consequences and to engage in an informed debate over certain questions such as: To whom should education be accountable? What form should accountability take? To what

degree are various forms of accountability equitable for all? To what degree is accountability an individual or collective responsibility?

A separate issue is uniformity and standardization. The more standards are specifically stated, the more they promote a uniform understanding of reality. This uniform understanding of reality is further strengthened by standardized instruction and assessment. In contrast, the more standards are posed as concepts, the more they allow for a diversity of opinion about the nature of reality. The diversity of opinion that is promoted through conceptual standards is enhanced by best-practice-based instruction that is assessed in multiple and authentic ways. The promotion of uniform views of reality requires control over teacher decision-making about curriculum, instruction, and assessment. In contrast, when diversity in thinking is promoted, teachers are empowered to make decisions about curriculum, instruction, and assessment. In the context of an increasingly pluralistic democratic society that is market driven, certain questions need to be addressed. Should children be subjected to a standards and accountability system that seeks to promote uniformity in knowledge and thinking? What are the consequences of a focus on uniformity and standardization for individuals and society?

Related to this issue is the fact that public education is inherently mass education. This raises the issue of whether technical standards and accountability systems are the only way in which the masses can be educated. Are there other options? Can public schools be redesigned so that the children of the general public can experience the progressive and, in some instances, radical education that occurs in some elite private schools? Scholars in the field of systems design (such as Bela H. Banathy [1991, 1996]) have formulated design processes in which schools can engage that can result in more **idealized educational systems.**

Idealized educational systems

School systems in which all of the stakeholders participate in the design and implementation of their educational system, which is based upon a shared vision and mission.

Finally, there is the issue of control. Who is being controlled in the different standards and accountability systems, and what is the nature and purpose of this control? Most individuals agree that in any system there is a need for a degree of control over the educational process and the individuals within the educational system. However, as seen, different standards and accountability systems have different views on the purpose and organization of control. As previously discussed, the current technical standards reforms are greatly influenced by the purposes of the business community and by those individuals who desire to construct a common culture based upon their own values. To accomplish these goals requires tight control over the educational processes and individuals within the school system. In contrast, the purposes of personal growth and the creation of a critical democratic citizenry that guide standards of complexity systems require less institutional control and a greater empowerment of the educational stakeholders. Elliot Eisner (1995) directly addresses this purpose in his statement that "learning to replicate known conventions is an important part of the *tactical outcomes* of education, but it is not adequate for achieving the *strategic aspirations* that we hold. These strategic aspirations require curricula and assessment policies that invite students to exercise judgment and to create outcomes that are not identical with those of their peers" (p. 762). To accomplish Eisner's purpose requires a different definition of control. In this case, teachers and students need to have more personal control over the learning process. The degree to which stakeholders are empowered in decision-making and implementation of the purpose of the system results in quite different organizational structures and role requirements. The more that individuals are empowered, the less institutional control exists over the individuals. However, in this case, as individuals acquire more power, they also acquire more responsibility for the success of the whole educational system.

Another aspect of educational control involves how much control individuals have over the learning process. Within technical standards systems, individuals, whether administrators, teachers, or students, are viewed as having control over their own teaching and learning. If test scores are deficient, the reason is either the teachers are not teaching effectively, or the students decide not to learn. This perception of an individual locus of control ignores the environmental factors that mediate all teaching and learning. Educational funding levels, resource availability, racism, sexism, school safety, and the socioeconomic condition of the community are only some of the factors that affect teaching and learning. Proponents of standards of complexity argue that individual teachers and students have little control over these factors; especially, if they are all in existence at the same time as

they are in many urban schools.

The issue of control also deals with how society views childhood. As Steinberg and Kincheloe (1997) point out, "childhood is a social and historical artifact, not simply a biological entity" (p. 1). This means that society determines how the roles played by children are defined. Critical theorists and others argue that if children are viewed as consumers and future workers, then education must be controlled so that children can learn how to play these roles. They further argue that these role attainment goals are achieved not only through the control of education by economic interests but also through the hidden corporate curriculum, directed at children, that permeates the media (Kenway & Bullen, 2001). Steinberg and Kincheloe (1997) also explain how various ideological and economic interests form power blocs, or alliances of interests, to promote certain cultural, political, social, and economic views of children (p. 7). This idea of power blocs attempting to influence society through children is evident in Gerald W. Bracey's (2003) commentary on the effects of No Child Left Behind, the attacks on the public schools, and the intrusion of business into education as it is now defined.

In relation to the control of children, certain critical questions need to be publicly answered. Should public schools be places where special interests can influence our children? Should the purposes of public education be centered on the preparation of children for predetermined economic and cultural roles in society, or should they be centered on the child's personal growth and development as a critical participant in American democracy?

A final aspect of control involves caring. To what degree is caring for children a relative concept? In other words, when an educational reform is designed and implemented, what is the level of acceptable loss in terms of student failure and attrition? How much collateral damage, in terms of dropouts and truncated educational experiences, is acceptable? To what degree is student failure a viable option? Should any educational reform be instituted that assumes some level of harm will occur to some anticipated number of students?

Glossary

Idealized educational systems—school systems in which all of the stakeholders participate in the design and implementation of their educational system, which is based upon a shared vision and mission.

Patterns of representation—one group's repetitious presentation of how another group is defined in its attempt to control that group.

References and Resources

Print Resources

Abrams, L. M., & Madaus, G. F. (2003, November). The lessons of high-stakes testing. *Educational Leadership, 61*(3), 31–35.

Allington, R. L. (Ed.). (2002). *Big brother and the national reading curriculum: How ideology trumped evidence.* Portsmouth, NH: Heinemann.

Amrein, A. L., & Berliner, D. C. (2002). *Figures calculated using 1998 data from KidsCount data book online.* Retrieved November 3, 2003, from http://www.aecf.org/kidscount/kc2001

Anderson, G. L., & Saavedra, E. (2002). School-based reform, leadership, and practitioner research: Mapping the terrain. *Scholar-Practitioner Quarterly, 1*(1), 23–38.

Applefield, J. M., Huber, R., & Moallem, M. (2000/2001). Constructivsm in theory and practice: Toward a better understanding. *The High School Journal, 84*(2), 35–66.

Archer, J. (2003a, September 24). Houston case offers lesson on dropouts: Lack of accurate figures called national problem. *Education Week, 23*(4), 1, 14–15.

Archer, J. (2003b, August 6). Urban schools chiefs complain of demands in 'impossible' roles. *Education Week, 22*(43), 1, 18–19.

Astuto, T. A., Clark, D. L., Read, A., McGree, K., & Ferandez, L. (1994). *Roots of reform: Challenging the assumptions that control change in education.* Bloomington, IN: Phi Delta Kappa, Educational Foundation.

Banathy, B.H. (1991). *Systems design of education: A journey to create the future.* Englewood Cliffs, NJ: Educational Technology.

Banathy, B. H. (1996). *Designing social systems in a changing world: A journey toward a creating society.* New York: Plenum.

Banks, J. A. (1994). *Multicultural education: Theory and practice (3rd ed.).* Boston: Allyn & Bacon.

Bauch, P. A., & Goldring, E. B. (1998). Parent-teacher participation in the context of school governance. *Peabody Journal of Education, 73*(1), 15–35.

Bennett, K. P., & LeCompte, M. D. (1990). *The way schools work: A sociological analysis of education.* New York: Longman.

Bentz, V. M. (2002). The mindful scholar-practitioner (MS-P). *Scholar-Practitioner Quarterly, 1*(1), 7–22.

Berkson, W. (1997). A place to stand: Breaking the impasse over standards. *Phi Delta Kappan, 79*(3), 207–211.

Berliner, D. C., & Biddle, B. J. (1996). *Manufactured crisis: Myths, fraud and the attack on American's schools.* Malibu, CA: Perseus.

Berry, K. (2001). Standards of complexity in a postmodern democracy. In J. L. Kincheloe, & D. Weil (Eds.), *Standards and schooling in the United States: An encyclopedia* (pp. 297–312. Santa Barbara, CA: ABC-CLIO.

Bertrand, L. (2001). Promoting student success through the mastery of the Texas assessment of academic skills. In R. A. Horn and J. L. Kincheloe (Eds.), *American standards: Quality education in a complex world—The Texas case* (131–140). New York: Peter Lang.

Bloom, B., Englelhart, A., Furst, W., Hill, W., & Krathwohl, C. (1956). *Taxonomy of educational objectives.* New York: McKay.

Bobbitt, F. (1918). *The curriculum.* New York: Houghton Mifflin.

Bourdieu. P., & Passeron, J. (1977). *Reproduction: In education, society, and culture.* Beverly Hills, CA: Sage.

Bracey, G. W. (1997). *Setting the record straight: Responses to misconceptions about public education in the United States.* Alexandria, VA: Association for Supervision and Curriculum Development.

Bracey, G. W. (1998). *Put to the test: An educator's and consumer's guide to standardized testing.* Bloomington, IN: Phi Delta Kappa International.

Bracey, G. W. (2000). *A short guide to standardized testing.* Bloomington, IN: Phi Delta Kappa Educational Foundation.

Bracey, G. W. (2002). *The war against America's public schools: Privatizing schools, commercializing education.* Boston: Allyn & Bacon.

Bracey, G. W. (2003). *On the death of childhood and the destruction of public schools.* Portsmouth, NH: Heinemann.

Brookings Institution. (2003, October 1). A new study reveals that homework in the United States is an easy load. Retrieved November 3, 2003 from http://www.brook.edu/comm/news/20031001brown.htm

Buell, J., & Kralovec, E. (2003, October 29). Lazy children or misplaced priorities? Homework, life, and educational excellence. *Education Week, 23*(9), 44.

Bush, G. (1991). *America 2000: An education strategy.* Washington, DC: U.S. Government Printing Office.

Business Roundtable. (1996). *A business leader's guide to setting academic standards.* Washington, DC: Author.

Callahan, R. E. (1962). *Education and the cult of efficiency: A study of the social forces that have shaped administration of the public schools.* Chicago: The University of Chicago Press.

Canady, R. L., & Rettig, M. D. (1996). *Teaching in the block: Strategies for engaging active learners.* Larchmont, NY: Eye on Education.

Cárdenas, J. A. (1998, October). School-student performance and accountability. *Intercultural Development Research Association Newsletter, 25*(9), 1–2, 17–19.

Carnevale, A. P., Gainer, L. J., & Meltzer, A. S. (1990). *Workplace basics: The essential skills employers want.* San Francisco: Jossey-Bass.

Chall, J. S. (1967). *Learning to read: The great debate.* New York: McGraw-Hill.

Chall, J. S. (2000). *The academic achievement challenge: What really works in the classroom?* New York: Guilford.

Charlesworth, R., Fleege, P. O., & Weitman, C. J. (1994). Research on the effects of group standardized testing on instruction, pupils, and teachers: New directions for policy. *Early Education and Development, 5*(3), 195–212.

Cheney, L. V. (1994, October 20). The end of history. *The Wall Street Journal.*

Cizek, G. J. (Ed.). (2001). *Setting performance standards: Concepts, methods, and perspectives.* Mahwah, NJ: Erlbaum.

Clarke, J. H., & Agne, R. M. (1997). *Interdisciplinary high school teaching: Strategies for integrated learning.* Boston: Allyn and Bacon.

Cochran-Smith, M., & Lytle, S. L. (1999). Relationships of knowledge and practice: Teacher learning communities. *Review of Research in Education, 24,* 249–305.

Cole, M. (1996). *Cultural psychology: A once and future discipline.* Cambridge, MA: Harvard University Press.

Cole, M., & Wertsch, J. V. (1996). Beyond the individual-social antimony in discussion of Piaget and Vygotsky. *Human Development, 39,* 250–256.

Creighton, T., & Young, M. (2003). A conversation with Fenwick English: Standards without standardization. *NCPEA Education Leadership Review, 4*(1), 33–36.

Cremin, L. (1989). *Popular education and its discontents.* New York: Harper and Row.

Crotty, M. (1998). *The foundations of social research: Meaning and perspective in the research process.* Thousand Oaks, CA: Sage Publications.

Crowson, R. L. (1998). Community empowerment and the public schools: Can educational professionalism survive? *Peabody Journal of Education, 73* (1), 56–68.

Daniels, H. (2001). *Vygotsky and pedagogy.* London: Routledge/Falmer.

Denzin, N. K., & Lincoln, Y. S. (1994). Introduction: Entering the field of qualitative research. In Denzin, N. K. & Lincoln, Y. S., (Eds). *Handbook of Qualitative Research.* Thousand Oaks: Sage.

Dewey, J. (1916). *Democracy and education.* New York: The Free Press.

Dewey, J. (1963/1938). *Experience and education.* New York: Macmillan/ Collier.

Dufour, R., & Eaker, R. (1998). *Professional learning communities at work: Best practices for enhancing student achievement.* Bloomington, IN: National Education Services.

Eisner, E. (1995). Standards for American schools: Help or hindrance? *Phi Delta Kappan, 76*(10), 758–764.

Elmore, R. F. (2003, November). A plea for strong practice. *Educational Leadership, 61*(3), 6–11.

Fisher, F. (2000). *Tall tales? Texas testing moves from the Pecos to Woebegon.* Unpublished manuscript.

Freeland, R. M., & Tucci, J. M. (2003, September 3). Out of school and unemployed: Why America must intensify its efforts to stem the dropout rate. *Education Week, 23*(1), 42.

Freire, P. (1985). *The politics of education: Culture, power and liberation.* New York: Bergin & Garvey.

Freire, P. (1996). *Pedagogy of the oppressed.* New York: Continuum.

Gaddy, B. B., Hall, T. W., & Marzano, R. J. (1996). *School wars: Resolving our conflicts over religion and values.* San Francisco: Jossey-Bass.

Galley, M. (2003 September 17). Texas principal posts test scores of classes. *Education Week, 23*(3), 3.

GI Forum, et al. v. Texas Education Agency et al....No. SA 97 CA 1278EP (W.D.Tex., January 6, 2000 memorandum opinion)

GI Forum, et al. v. Texas Education Agency et al....No. SA 97 CA 1278EP (W.D.Tex., November 8, 1999 Plainiffs' Post Trial Brief)

Giroux, H. (1988). *Teachers as intellectuals: Toward a critical pedagogy of learning.* MA: Bergin & Garvey.

Giroux, H. (1993). Teachers as transformative intellectuals. In H. S. Shapiro, & D. E. Purpel (Eds.). *Critical social issues in American education* (pp. 273–277). New York: Longman.

Giroux, H. A. (1996). *Living dangerously: Multiculturalism and the politics of difference.* New York: Peter Lang.

Goodman, K. (1986). *What's whole in whole language?* Portsmouth, NH: Heinemann.

Gould, S. J. (1981). *The mismeasure of man.* New York: W. W. Norton.

Gratz, D. B. (2000). High standards for whom? *Phi Delta Kappan, 81*(9), 681–684.

Greene, M. (1988). *The dialectic of freedom.* New York: Teachers College Press.

Grenz, S. J. (1996). *A primer on postmodernism.* Grand Rapids, MI: Eerdmans.

Haladyna, T., Nolen, S. B., & Haas, N. S. (1991). Raising standardized achievement scores and the origins of test score pollution. *Educational Researcher, 20*(5), 2–7.

Hambleton, R. K. (2001). Setting performance standards on educational assessments and criteria for evaluating the process. In G. J. Cizek (Ed.), *Setting performance standards: Concepts, methods, and perspectives* (pp. 89–116). Mahwah, NJ: Erlbaum.

Haney, W. (2000). The Texas miracle in education. *Education Policy Analysis Archives,* 8(41). Retrieved August 10, 2003 from http://olam.ed.asu.edu/epaa/v8n41

Hartocollis, A. (1999, December 12). Crossed fingers: Liar, liar, pants on fire. *New York Times.* Retrieved November 3, 2003, from http://www.nytimes.com

Hartocollis, A. (2000, May 3). Nine educators accused of encouraging students to cheat. *New York Times.* Retrieved November 3, 2003, from http://www.nytimes.com

Herrnstein, R. J., & Murray, C. (1994). *The bell curve: Intelligence and class structure in American Life.* New York: Free Press.

Hirsch, E. D., Jr. (1988). *Cultural literacy: What every American needs to know.* New York: Vintage.

Hirsch, E. D., Jr., Kett, J. F., & Trefil, J. (1988). *The dictionary of cultural literacy.* Boston: Houghton Mifflin.

Hoff, D. J. (2003, November 5). Flaws could spell trouble for N.Y. regents exams. *Education Week, 23*(10), 22, 27.

Hoffman, J.V., Assaf, L. C., & Paris, S. G. (2001). High-stakes testing in reading: Today in Texas tomorrow? *Reading Teacher, 54*(5), 482–492.

Hofstadter, R. (1964). *Anti-intellectualism in American life.* New York: Knopf.

Horn, R. A. (2001a). A post-formal conversation about standardization and accountability in Texas. In J. L. Kincheloe, & D. Weil (Eds.), *Standards and schooling in the United States: An encyclopedia* (pp. 1057–1074). Santa Barbara, CA: ABC-CLIO.

Horn, R. A. (2001b). Is Texas failing to equitably educate minorities? In R. A. Horn, & J. L. Kincheloe (Eds.), *American standards: Quality education in a complex world—The Texas case* (pp. 159–174). New York: Peter Lang.

Horn, R. A. (2001c). Kids, the court, and the state of Texas: The legal challenge to the TAAS . In R. A. Horn & J. L. Kincheloe (Eds.), *American standards: Quality education in a complex world—The Texas case* (pp. 281–306). New York: Peter Lang.

Horn, R. A., Jr. (2002). *Understanding educational reform: A reference handbook.* Denver, CO: ABC-CLIO.

Horn, R. A., Jr. (2003). The Texas model of high-stakes assessment: Implications for teacher practice in Pennsylvania. *Pennsylvania Educational Leadership, 22*(2), 6–16.

Hunter, M. (1982). *Mastery teaching.* El Segundo, CA: TIP.

Jacobson, L. (2003, July 9). New report tracks states' preschool learning standards. *Education Week, 22*(42), 16.

Jaeger, R. M. (1991). Selection of judges for standard setting. *Educational Measurement Issues and Practice,* 10, 3–6, 10.

Jencks, C. (1972). *Inequality: A reassessment of the effect of family and schooling in America.* New York: Basic Books.

Jencks, C., & Phillips, M. (Eds.). (1998). *The black-white test score gap.* Washington, DC: Brookings Institute.

Jenlink, P. M. (2002). The scholar-practitioner as bricoleur. *Scholar-Practitioner Quarterly, 1*(2), 3–6.

Jenlink, P., & Carr, A. A. (1996). *Conversation as a medium for change in education. Educational Technology, 36* (1), 31–38.

Jensen, A. R. (1974). How biased are culture-loaded tests? *Genetic Psych, Monographs 90*, 185–244.

Jensen, A. R. (1980). *Bias in mental testing.* New York: Free Press.

Jerald, C. (2003, November). Beyond the rock and the hard place. *Educational Leadership, 61*(3), 12–17.

Johnson, J. (2003, November). What does the public say about accountability? *Educational Leadership, 61*(3), 36–40.

Johnson, R. (1999, October). Attrition rates in Texas public high schools still high. *Intercultural Development Research Association Newsletter, 26*(9), 1–2, 8–15.

Jones, M. G., Jones, B. D., Hardin, B., & Chapman, L. (1999). The impact of high stakes testing on teachers and students in North Carolina. *Phi Delta Kappan, 81*(3), 199–203.

Jorgenson, O., & Vanosdall, R. (2002). The death of science? What we risk in our rush toward standardized testing and the three R's. *Phi Delta Kappan, 83*(8), 601–605.

Kane, M. T. (2001). So much remains the same: Conception and status on validation in setting standards. In G. J. Cizek, (Ed.), *Setting performance standards: Concepts, methods, and perspectives* (pp. 53–88). Mahwah, NJ: Erlbaum.

Kazdin, A. E. (1989). *Behavior modification in applied settings.* Pacific Grove, CA: Brooks/Cole.

Kincheloe, J. L. (1991). *Teachers as researchers: Qualitative inquiry as a path to empowerment.* Philadelphia, PA: Falmer.

Kincheloe, J. L. (1993). *Toward a critical politics of teacher thinking: Mapping the postmodern.* Westport, CT: Bergin & Garvey.

Kincheloe, J. L. (1998a). Critical research in science education. In Fraser, B. & Tobin, K., (Eds). *International handbook of science education* (pp. 1191–1205). Boston: Kluwer.

Kincheloe, J. L. (Ed.). (1998b). *The Post-formal thinking defined.* New York: Guilford.

Kincheloe, J. L. (2001a). Developing a curriculum of complexity: Substituting connectedness for fragmentation. In J. L. Kincheloe, & D. Weil (Eds.), *Standards and schooling in the United States: An encyclopedia* (pp. 267–296). Santa Barbara, CA: ABC-CLIO.

Kincheloe, J. L. (2001b). From positivism to an epistemology of complexity: Grounding rigorous teaching. In J. L. Kincheloe & D. Weil (Eds.), *Standards and schooling in the United States: An encyclopedia* (pp. 325–396). Santa Barbara, CA: ABC-CLIO.

Kincheloe, J. L. (2001c). Introduction: Hope in the shadows—Reconstructing the debate over educational standards. In J. L. Kincheloe & D. Weil (Eds.), *Standards and schooling in the United States: An encyclopedia* (pp. 1–104). Santa Barbara, CA: ABC-CLIO.

Kincheloe, J. L., & Steinberg, S. R. (1997). *Changing multiculturalism: New times, new curriculum.* London: Open University Press.

Kincheloe, J. L., & Steinberg, S. R. (Eds.). (1998). *Students as researchers: Creating classrooms that matter.* Bristol, PA: Falmer.

Kincheloe, J. L., Steinberg, S. R., & Gresson III, A. D. (Eds.). (1996). *Measured lies: The bell curve examined.* New York: St. Martin's Press.

Kincheloe, J. L., Steinberg, S. R., & Hinchey, P. (Eds.). (1999). *The Post-formal reader: Cognition and education.* New York: Garland.

Klein, S., Hamilton, L., McCaffrey, D., & Stecher, B. (2000). *What do test scores in Texas tell us?* Santa Monica, CA: RAND.

Kliebard, H. M. (1995). *The struggle for the American curriculum: 1893–1958* (2nd Ed). New York: Routledge.

Kohn, A. (1993). *Punished by rewards: The problem with gold stars, incentive plans, A's, praise, and other bribes.* Boston: Houghton Mifflin.

Kohn, A., & Shannon, P. (Eds.). (2002). *Education, Inc.: Turning learning into a business.* Portsmouth, NH: Heinemann.

Koretz, D. M. (1995). Sometimes a cigar is only a cigar, and often a test is only a test. In D. Ravitch (Ed.)., *Debating the future of American education: Do we need national standards and assessments?* (pp. 154–166). Washington, DC: The Brookings Institution.

Kornhaber, M. L., & Orfield, G. (2001). High-stakes testing policies: Examining their assumptions and consequences. In G. Orfield, & M. L. Kornhaber (Eds.), *Raising standards or raising barriers: Inequality and high-stakes testing in public education* (pp. 1–18). New York: The Century Foundation Press.

Lagemann, E. C. (2000). *An elusive science: The troubling history of education research.* Chicago: The University of Chicago Press.

Lather, P. (1991). *Getting smart: Feminist research and pedagogy with/in the postmodern.* New York: Routledge.

Lave, J. (1988). *Cognition in practice: Mind, mathematics and culture in everyday life.* Cambridge, MA: Cambridge University Press.

Lave, J., & Wenger, E. (1991). *Situated learning: Legitimate peripheral participation.* New York: Cambridge University Press.

Levin, H. M. (2001). High-stakes testing and economic productivity. In Orfield, G., & Kornhaber, M. L. (eds.), *Raising standards or raising barri-*

ers? Inequality and high-stakes testing in American education, pp. 39–50. New York: The Century Foundation Press.

Levi-Strauss, C. (1966). *The savage mind.* Chicago: The University of Chicago Press.

Linn, R. L. (1996). Work readiness assessment: Questions of validity. In Resnick, L., & Wirt, J. (eds.), *Linking school and work: Roles for standards and assessment,* pp. 245–266). San Francisco: Jossey-Bass.

Longstreet, W. S. (1973). *Beyond Jencks: The myth of equal schooling.* Washington, DC: Association for Supervision and Curriculum Development.

Low, R., & Horn, R. A. (2001). The administrator's caper. In Horn, R. A. (Ed.), *American standards: Quality education in a complex world—The Texas case* (141–148) New York: Peter Lang.

Lowery, S., & Buck, J. (2002). Three decades of educational reform in Texas: Putting the pieces together. In R. A. Horn & J. L. Kincheloe (Eds.), *American standards: Quality education in a complex world—The Texas case* (pp. 267–280). New York: Peter Lang.

Madaus, G., & Clarke, M. (2001). The adverse impact of high-stakes testing on minority students: Evidence from one hundred years of test data. (2001). In G. Orfield, & M. L. Kornhaber (Eds.), *Raising standards or raising barriers: Inequality and high-stakes testing in public education* (pp. 85–106). New York: The Century Foundation Press.

Marshak, D. (2003, November). No child left behind: A foolish race into the past. *Phi Delta Kappan, 85*(3), 229–231.

Mawhinney, Hanne B. (1998). School wars or school transformation: Professionalizing teaching and involving communities. *Peabody Journal of Education, 73* (1), 36–55.

McNeil, L. M. (2000). *Contradictions of school reform: Educational costs of standardized testing.* New York: Routledge.

Meichenbaum, D. (1979). *Cognitive-behavior modification: An integrative approach.* New York: Plenum.

Meier, D. (2000). *Will standards save public education?* Boston: Beacon Press.

Mezirow, J. (2000). *Learning as transformation: Critical perspectives on a theory in progress.* New York: Jossey-Bass.

Murnane, R. J., Willett, J. B., & Tyler, J. H. (2000). Who benefits from obtaining a GED? Evidence from High School and Beyond. *Review of Economics and Statistics, 82*(1), 23–37.

Muth, R. (2002). Scholar-practitioner goals, practices, and outcomes: What students and faculty need to know and be able to do. *Scholar-Practitioner Quarterly, 1*(1), 67–87.

National Center on Education and the Economy (1998). *New standards: Performance standards and assessments for the schools.* Washington, D. C.: Author.

National Center for History in the Schools (1996) *National standards for United States history: Exploring the American experience.* Los Angeles, CA: Author.

National Commission on Excellence in Education (1983). *A nation at risk: The report of the national commission on excellence in education.* Washington, DC: U.S. Department of Education.

National Council for the Social Studies (1994). *Expectations of excellence: Curriculum standards for social studies.* Washington, DC: National Council for the Social Studies.

National Council of Teachers of English & International Reading Association (1996). *Standards for the English language arts.* Urbana, IL: NCTE and IRA.

National Council of Teachers of Mathematics (1989). *Curriculum and evaluation standards for school mathematics.* Reston, VA: National Council of Teachers of Mathematics.

Nash, G. B., Crabtree, C., & Dunn, R. E. (2000). *History on trial: Culture wars and the teaching of the past.* New York: Vintage.

Natriello, G. (1996). Diverting attention from conditions in American schools. *Educational Researcher, 25,* 7–9.

Natriello, G., & Pallas, A. M. (2001). The development and impact of high-stakes testing. In G. Orfield, & M. L. Kornhaber (Eds.), *Raising standards or raising barriers: Inequality and high-stakes testing in public education* (pp. 19–38). New York: The Century Foundation Press.

Neill, D. M., & Medina, N. J. (1989), Standardized testing: Harmful to educational health. *Phi Delta Kappan, 70*(9), 688–697.

Neill, M. (2000). What is the purpose of assessment? In K. Swope, & B. Miner (Eds.). *Failing our kids: Why the testing craze won't fix our schools* (pp. 102–103). Milwaukee, WI: Rethinking Schools.

Neill, M. (2003, November). Leaving children behind: How No Child Left Behind will fail our children. *Phi Delta Kappan, 85*(3), 225–228.

New Standards. (n.d.). Retrieved November 3, 2003 from http://www.ncrel.org/drs/areas/issues/methods/assment/as7nsp.htm

Noddings, N. (1997). Thinking about standards. *Phi Delta Kappan, 79*(3), 184–189.

Ogawa, R. (1998). Organizing parent-teacher relations around the work of teaching. *Peabody Journal of Education, 73* (I), 6–14.

Ohanian, S. (1999). *One size fits few: The folly of educational standards.* Portsmouth, NH: Heinemann.

Ohanian, S. (2000). Goals 2000: What's in a name. *Phi Delta Kappan, 81*(5), 344–355.

Orfield, G., & Kornhaber, M. L. (Eds.). (2001). *Raising standards or raising barriers? Inequality and high-stakes testing in public education.* New York: Century Foundation Press.

Orfield, G., & Wald, J. (2000). Testing unequal impact. In K. Swope & B. Miner (Eds). *Failing our kids: Why the testing craze won't fix our schools* (pp. 74–75). Milwaukee, WI: Rethinking Schools.

Ornstein, A. C., & Hunkins, F. P. (Eds.). (1998). *Curriculum: Foundations, principles, and issues (3rd Ed.).* Needham Heights, MA: Allyn and Bacon.

Palmer, D. D. (1997). *Structuralism and poststructuralism for beginners.* New York: Writers and Readers.

Pedulla, J. J. (2003, November). State-mandated testing: What do teachers think? *Educational Leadership, 61*(3), 42–46.

Peterson, B., & Neill, M. (2001). Alternatives to standardized testing. In J. L. Kincheloe, & D. Weil (Eds.), *Standards and schooling in the United States: An encyclopedia* (pp. 983–994). Santa Barbara, CA: ABC-CLIO.

Pinar, W., Reynolds, W., Slattery, P., & Taubman, P. (1995). *Understanding curriculum.* New York: Peter Lang.

Popham, W. J. (2001). *The truth about testing: An educator's call to action.* Alexandria, VA: Association for Supervision and Curriculum Development.

Porter, A. E. (1995). The uses and misuse of opportunity-to-learn standards. In Ravitch, D. (Ed.). *Debating the future of American education: Do we need national standards and assessments?* (pp. 40–65). Washington, D C: The Brookings Institution.

Powell, J. (1998). *Postmodernism for beginners.* New York: Writers and Readers.

Public Agenda (2003). Where we are now: 12 things you need to know about public opinion and public schools. Retrieved November 3, 2003, from http://www.publicagenda.org

Ravitch, D. (2000). *Left back: A century of failed school reforms.* New York: Simon & Schuster.

Raymond, M. R., & Reid, J. B. (2001). Who made thee a judge? Selecting and training participants for standard setting. In G. J. Cizek (Ed.), *Setting performance standards: Concepts, methods, and perspectives* (pp. 89–116). Mahwah, NJ: Erlbaum.

Reeves, D. B. (2002). *The leader's guide to standards: A blueprint for educational equity and excellence.* San Francisco, CA: Jossey-Bass.

Reid, K. S. (2003, September 3). Florida, Texas retain 3rd graders with poor reading scores. *Education Week, 23*(1), 25.

Resnick, L., & Nolan, K. (1995). Standards for education. In Ravitch, D. (Ed.). *Debating the future of American education: Do we need national standards and assessments?* (pp. 94–119). Washington, D C: The Brookings Institution.

Reyes, P., Scribner, J. D., & Scribner, A. P. (1999). *Lessons from high-performing Hispanic schools: Creating learning communities.* New York: Teachers College Press.

Rosenshine. B. (1988). Explicit teaching. In D. Berliner, & B. Rosenshine (Eds.). *Talks to teachers* (pp. 75–92). New York: Random House.

Saavedra, E. (1995). *Teacher transformation: Creating texts and contexts in study groups.* Unpublished doctoral dissertation, University of Arizona, Tucson.

Sacks, P. (1999). *Standardized minds: The high price of America's testing culture and what we can do to change it.* Cambridge, MA: Perseus.

Saltman, K. J. (2000). *Collateral damage: Corporatizing public schools—A threat to democracy.* New York: Rowman & Littlefield.

Sauer, R. T. (2003, May 21. Jencks reassessed, one career later. *Education Week, 22*(43), 32, 34.

Schlesinger, A. M., Jr. (1998). *The disuniting of America: Reflections on a multicultural society.* New York: W. W. Norton.

Secretary's Commission on Achieving Necessary Skills, United States Department of Labor (1991, June). *What work requires of schools: A SCANS report for America 2000.* Washington, DC: U.S. Government Printing Office.

Sergiovanni, T. J. (1992). *Moral leadership: Getting to the heart of school reform.* San Francisco, CA: Jossey-Bass.

Sergiovanni, T. J. (1994). *Building community in schools.* San Francisco, CA: Jossey-Bass.

Shedd, J. B., & Bacharach, S. B. (1991). *Tangled hierarchies: Teachers as professionals and the management of schools.* San Francisco: Jossey-Bass.

Sheehy, M. (2002). Illuminating constructivism: Structure, discourse, and subjectivity in a middle school classroom. *Reading Research Quarterly, 37*(3), 278–308.

Shipps, D., & Firestone, W. A. (2003, June 18). Juggling accountabilities. *Education Week, 22*(41), 45, 56.

Shor, I. (1992). Empowering education: Critical teaching for social change. Chicago: University of Chicago Press.

Sizer, T. R. (1984). *Horace's compromise: The dilemma of the American high school.* New York: Houghton Mifflin.

Sizer, T. R. (1992). *Horace's school: Redesigning the American high school.* New York: Houghton Mifflin.

Sizer, T. R. (1996). *Horace's hope: What works for the American high school.* Boston: Houghton Mifflin.

Smith, G. A. (2000). Place-based education: Learning to be where we are. *Phi Delta Kappan, 83*(8), 584–594.

Smith, G. A., & Williams, D. (Eds.). (1999). *Ecological education in action: On weaving education, culture, and the environment.* New York: State University of New York Press.

Smith, M. L. (1991). Put to the test: The effects of external testing on teachers. *Educational Researcher, 20*(5), 8–11.

Smith, M. L., & Rottenburg, C. (1991). Unintended consequences of external testing in elementary schools. *Educational Measurement: Issues and Practice, 10*(4), 7–11.

Spring, J. (1989). *The sorting machine revisited: National educational policy since 1945.* New York: Longman.

Spring, J. (2001). *Deculturalization and the struggle for equality: A brief history of the education of dominated cultures in the United States (3rd ed.).* New York: McGraw-Hill.

Steinberg, S. R., & Kincheloe, J. L. (1997). Introduction: No more secrets— Kinderculture, information saturation, and the postmodern childhood. In S. R. Steinberg, & Kincheloe, J. L. (Eds.), *Kinderculture: The corporate construction of childhood* (pp. 1–30). Boulder, CO: Westview.

Stiggins, R. (2002). Assessment crisis: The absence of assessment for learning. *Phi Delta Kappan, 85,* 758–765.

Suval, J. (1999, April 12). Dropout rates hard to figure, officials note. *The Monitor.*

Swope, K., & Miner, B. (Eds.) (2000a). *Failing our kids: Why the testing craze won't fix our schools.* Milwaukee, WI: Rethinking Schools.

Swope, K., & Miner, B. (2000b). Standardized tests: Common questions. In Swope, K. & Miner, B. (Eds.). *Failing our kids: Why the testing craze won't fix our schools* (pp. 10–12) Milwaukee, WI: Rethinking Schools.

Symcox, L. (2002). *Whose history? The struggle for national standards in American classrooms.* New York: Teachers College Press.

Taylor, F. W. (1911). *The principles of scientific management.* New York: Harper.

Texas Education Agency (1998). *Texas dropout rates by ethnicity* [On-line]. Available: http//www.tea.state.tx.us/html

Texas Education Agency (2003). How are teachers held accountable for student performance. Retrieved November 3, 2003 from http://www.tea.state.tx.us/PDAS/cat/studperf.html

Thornburg, D. (2002). *The new basics: Education and the future of work in the telematic age.* Alexandria, VA: Association for Supervision and Curriculum Development.

Thurlow, M. L., & Ysseldyke, J. E. (2001). Standards setting challenges for special populations. In G. J. Cizek (Ed.), *Setting performance standards: Concepts, methods, and perspectives* (pp. 387–410). Mahwah, NJ: Erlbaum.

Tönnies, F. (1957, originally published in 1887). (C. P. Loomis, ed. and trans.) *Gemeinschaft und Gesellschaft [Community and society].* New York: HarperCollins.

Trotter, A. (2003, October 22). Testing aid for some students leads to scoring flap in Maryland. *Education Week, 23*(8), 12.

Tucker, M. S., & Codding, J. B. (1998). *Standards for our schools: How to set them, measure them, and reach them.* San Francisco, CA: Jossey-Bass.

United States Congress (103rd, second session) (1994). *Goals 2000: Educate America Act: Conference report (to accompany H.R. 1804).* Washington, DC: U.S. G.P.O., 1994.

United States Department of Education (2001). No Child Left Behind Act. Public Law print of PL 107–110, Title IX. Retrieved August 10, 2003, http://www.ed.gov/legislation/ESEA02/pg107.html

United States Department of Education (2002). Educational Sciences Reform Act of 2002. Public Law print of H. 3801. Retrieved August 10, 2003 from http://www.ed.gov/legislation/EdSciencesRef/PL107–279.pdf

Valenzuela, A. (1999). *Subtractive schooling: U. S.-Mexican youths and the politics of caring.* Albany. NY: State University of New York Press.

Valenzuela, A. (2000). The significance of the TAAS test for Mexican immigrant and Mexican-American adolescents: A cast study. *Hispanic Journal of Behavioral Sciences, 22*(4), 524–539.

Viadero, D. (2000, March). Lags in minority achievement defy traditional explanations. *Education Week.* Retrieved August 10, 2003 from http://www.edweek.org/ew/ewstory.cfm?slug=28causes.h19

Walsh, M. (2003, August 6). Companies jump on 'No Child Left Behind' bandwagon. *Education Week, 22*(43), 8.

Watson, D. L., & Tharp, R. G. (1997). *Self-directed behavior: Self-modification for personal adjustment.* Pacific Grove, CA: Brooks/Cole.

Wertsch, J. V. (1985). *Vygotsky and the social formation of mind.* Cambridge, MA: Harvard University Press.

Wheelock, A. (2003, November). Myopia in Massachusetts. *Educational Leadership, 61*(3), 50–54.

Wheelock, A. Bebell, D. J., & Haney, W. (2000). What can student drawings tell us about high-stakes testing in Massachusetts? *Teachers College Record.* Retrieved November 3, 2003 from http://www.tcrecord.org/Content.asp?ContentID=10634

Wilde, S. (2002). *Testing and standards: A brief encyclopedia.* Portsmouth, NH: Heinemann.

Woolfolk, A. E. (2004). *Educational psychology (9th Ed.).* Boston, MA: Allyn & Bacon.

Yardley, J. (2000, October 30). Critics say a focus on test scores is overshadowing education in Texas. *New York Times,* 14.

Zehr, M. A. (2003, September 3). Massachusetts teachers learn hard lesson: Flunk the English test, get fired. *Education Week, 23*(1), 22.

Nonprint Resources

The following individuals and organizations represent various positions and provide information on the issue of standards and accountability.

Alfie Kohn
    http://www.alfiekohn.org

Association for Supervision and Curriculum Development (ASCD)
    1703 North Beauregard Street
    Alexandria, VA 22311–1714
    800–933–2723
    http://www.ascd.org

Brookings Institution
    http://www.brook.edu

Center for Performance Assessment
    1660 S. Albion St, Suite 1002
    Denver, CO 80222
    800–844–6599

Center for Research on Evaluation, Standards, and Student Testing (CRESST)
    CRESST/University of California, Los Angeles
    P. O. Box 951522
    300 Charles E. Young Drive
    North Los Angeles, CA 90095–1522
    310–206–1532
    http://cresst96.cse.ucla.edu/index.htm

The Civil Rights Project, Harvard University
    124 Mt. Auburn Street, Suite 400 South

Cambridge, MA 02138
(617)496–6367
http://www.law.harvard.edu/civilrights/

Coalition for Essential Schools
1814 Franklin St. Suite 700
Oakland, CA 94612
510–433–1451
http://www.essentialschools.org

Council of Chief State School Officers
One Massachusetts Avenue NW , Suite 700
Washington, DC 20001–1431
1–202–336–7000
http://www.ccsso.org/

Education Commission of the States
http://www.ecs.org

Education Week
Suite 100
6935 Arlington Road
Bethesada, MD 20814–5233
(800) 346–1834
http://www.edweek.org.

Gerald Bracey
http://www.america-tomorrow.com/bracey.

Grass Roots Innovative Policy Program (GRIPP) of the Applied
Research Center
3781 Broadway St.
Oakland, CA 94611
510–653–3415

The Heritage Foundation
214 Massachusetts Ave NE
Washington DC 20002–4999
(202) 546–4400
http://www.heritage.org

International Center for Educational Accountability
http://www.edaccountability.org

International Reading Association
800 Barksdale, P.O. Box 8139
Newark, DE 18714
302–731–1600
http://www.reading.org/advocacy/policies/high_stakes.pdf

Learning Research and Development Center of the University of
Pittsburgh

http://www.lrdc.pitt.edu

National Alliance of Black School Educators
http://www.nabse.org

National Assessment of Educational Progress (NAEP)
http://nces.ed.gov/nationsreportcard/site/home.asp

National Association for the Education of Young Children
1509 16th St. NW
Washington, DC 20036
800–424–2460

National Association of Administrators
http://www.aasa.org

National Association of Elementary School Principals
http://www.naesp.org

National Association of Secondary School Principals
http://www.nassp.org

National Board for Professional Teaching Standards
26555 Evergreen Road, Suite 400
Southfield, MI 48076
248–351–4444
http://www.nbpts.org

National Center for Educational Accountability
http://www.measuretolearn.org

National Center for Educational Statistics
http://nces.ed.gov

National Center for Fair and Open Testing (Fair Test)
342 Broadway
Cambridge, MA 02139
617–864–4810
http://www.fairtest.org

National Center for Research on Evaluation, Standards, and Student
Testing (CRESST)
www.cresst96.cse.ucla.edu

National Coalition of Education Activists
P.O. Box 679
Rhinebeck, NY 12572
914–876–4580

National Council of Teachers of English (NCTE)
1111 W. Kenyon Rd.
Urbana, IL 61801
http://www.ncte.org/resolutions/highstakes1999.html

National Council on Teacher Quality
http://www.nctq.org

National Education Association
1202 Sixteenth Street, NW
Washington, DC 20036
202–822–7200
http://www.nea.org/

National Research Council's Board on Testing and Assessment
http://www4.nationalacademies.org/cbsse/bota.nsf

National Science Teachers Association
http://www.nsta.org/nclb

No Child Left Behind
http://www.ed.gov/inits/nclb/index/html

North Central Regional Educational Laboratory
info@ncrel.org
http://www.ncrel.org

Pacific Research Institute
http://www.pacificresearch.org

Rethinking Schools
1001 E. Keefe Ave.,
Milwaukee, WI 53212
800–669–4192
www.rethinkingschools.org

Thomas B. Fordham Foundation
1627 K Street, NW , Suite 600
Washington, DC 20006
(202) 223–5452
http://www.edexcellence.net

United States Department of Education
400 Maryland Ave., SW
Washington, DC 20202–0498
(800) 872–5327
http://www.ed.gov/

The following websites provide information specifically on the influence of business in public education.

Adbusters
http://www.adbusters.org

Center for a New American Dream
http://www.newdream.org

Center for the Analysis of Commercialism in Schools

http://www.schoolcommercialism.org

Commercial Alert
http://www.commercialalert.org

Corporate Watch
http://www.corpwatch.org

No Logo
http://www.nolog.com

National Center on Education and the Economy: The New Standards
700 11th Street, NW, Suite 750
Washington, DC 20001
202–783–3668
http://www.ncee.org

Peter Lang
PRIMERS
in Education

Peter Lang Primers are designed to provide a brief and concise introduction or supplement to specific topics in education. Although sophisticated in content, these primers are written in an accessible style, making them perfect for undergraduate and graduate classroom use. Each volume includes a glossary of key terms and a References and Resources section.

Other published and forthcoming volumes cover such topics as:

- Standards
- Popular Culture
- Critical Pedagogy
- Literacy
- Higher Education
- John Dewey
- Feminist Theory and Education
- Studying Urban Youth Culture
- Multiculturalism through Postformalism
- Creative Problem Solving
- Teaching the Holocaust
- Piaget and Education
- Deleuze and Education
- Foucault and Education

Look for more Peter Lang Primers to be published soon. To order other volumes, please contact our Customer Service Department:

> 800-770-LANG (within the US)
> 212-647-7706 (outside the US)
> 212-647-7707 (fax)

To find out more about this and other Peter Lang book series, or to browse a full list of education titles, please visit our website:

www.peterlangusa.com